The Debauchee by Aphra Behn

or, The Credulous Cuckold

A COMEDY

Aphra Behn was a prolific and well established writer but facts about her remain scant and difficult to confirm. What can safely be said though is that Aphra Behn is now regarded as a key English playwright and a major figure in Restoration theatre

Aphra was born into the rising tensions to the English Civil War. Obviously a time of much division and difficulty as the King and Parliament, and their respective forces, came ever closer to conflict.

There are claims she was a spy, that she travelled abroad, possibly as far as Surinam.

By 1664 her marriage was over (though by death or separation is not known but presumably the former as it occurred in the year of their marriage) and she now used Mrs Behn as her professional name.

Aphra now moved towards pursuing a more sustainable and substantial career and began work for the King's Company and the Duke's Company players as a scribe.

Previously her only writing had been poetry but now she would become a playwright. Her first, "The Forc'd Marriage", was staged in 1670, followed by "The Amorous Prince" (1671). After her third play, "The Dutch Lover", Aphra had a three year lull in her writing career. Again it is speculated that she went travelling again, possibly once again as a spy.

After this sojourn her writing moves towards comic works, which prove commercially more successful. Her most popular works included "The Rover" and "Love-Letters Between a Nobleman and His Sister" (1684–87).

With her growing reputation Aphra became friends with many of the most notable writers of the day. This is The Age of Dryden and his literary dominance.

From the mid 1680's Aphra's health began to decline. This was exacerbated by her continual state of debt and descent into poverty.

Aphra Behn died on April 16th 1689, and is buried in the East Cloister of Westminster Abbey. The inscription on her tombstone reads: "Here lies a Proof that Wit can never be Defence enough against Mortality." She was quoted as stating that she had led a "life dedicated to pleasure and poetry."

Index of Contents
ACT FIRST
Scene I
Scene II
ACT SECOND

Scene I
Scene II
ACT THIRD
Scene I
ACT FOURTH
Scene I
ACT FIFTH
Scene I
Aphra Behn – A Short Biography
Aphra Behn – A Concise Bibliography

ACT FIRST

SCENE I

Enter **CARELESS** and **WATT**

CARELESS
Watt, have you deliver'd the Letter, as I order'd you?

WATT
Yes, Sir, I have to your Uncles Friend Mr Save-all, but he says, he has made your peace so often and to so little purpose, that he now absolutely despairs of a Reconciliation between you.

CARELESS
But then thou shouldst have told him, I wou'd not take that for an answer.

WATT
Then he wou'd have answer'd me, Let your precious Master take his course, for he is like to have no better answer.

CARELESS
Couldst thou not tell him again, that I have taken all the Courses, a young Gentleman can, to maintain himself like one; but they are all run out, and I have not one trick to manage, and may perish unless that damn'd Uncle of mine, set me up again, nor know I how to arrive to that but through his Intercession.

WATT
Puh, Sir, then I know what he wou'd have told me again, and muster'd up all your Vices: then that this same Uncle (so despis'd a thing) before he discarded you, had releast you out of Prison, within the space of Thirteen months, a Dozen times.

CARELESS
Well, Coxcomb, that was not once a Month then. Why shou'd he upbraid me with it? I am sure 'twas I that suffer'd for't, and so you might have told him.

WATT

Yes, and then he wou'd have answered me, that your extravagant courses have cost your Uncle at least Fifteen hundred Pounds, and upon your last debauch (when he resolv'd never to concern himself for you again, about a year ago) he cast another Five hundred Pound after you, with this Proviso that you shou'd never trouble him any more; and at last finding you incorrigible, he Marry'd on purpose to disinherit you.

CARELESS
Ay, that damn'd Marriage has ruin'd me—but, damn it, let it go, and let my Uncle go to the Devil, and let Save-all go, and be damn'd for a Cynical Ass as he is.—I confess he has by his formal Solicitation, made up breaches between my Uncle and me, at least a Score of times, what a Devil had it been for him to have try'd his Interest for me once more?

WATT
I wish you wou'd consider what is to be done, for your own sake, besides you ought to take some care of me your Creature, that have stuck to you through all Fortunes, to maintain and keep up your Gallantry, and think in time before these Cloths are worn out, for you'll find it somewhat difficult to Equip your self again.

CARELESS
I care not, I will not give my self one Minutes trouble about it, I'll rather dye here in New Alsatia, or sell my self a Slave to the Galleys. Consider quoth a?—what shou'd I consider?

WATT
Consider your poor Whore Sir, for she (as you have manag'd her) is in a worse Case than your self; her Cloths grow somewhat shabby.

CARELESS
Ay there's it, I wou'd willingly do somewhat for her, but how the Devil knows.—Have I not already done all that possibly can be done by a distressed hopeless heir?

WATT
Has the Die quite fail'd you, and all the Cheats that thereupon depend? Your Marrabone bowling Booties forsaken you? your Tennis Court Betting? your Cock-Pit Cozenages too? and all your Arts of borrowing?

CARELESS
All, all Arts are quite confounded.

WATT
I wonder your Father shou'd leave you nothing to live upon but Wit, and that not for life.

CARELESS
Hold thy peace;—I am contriving a way how (tho it cost me my life,) to disgrace my Uncle.

WATT
There's a Plot! I beseech you think of your poor Whore, Sir—what do you think will become of her, if you shou'd cast away your self?

CARELESS

Thou knowst I must leave her once.

WATT
If you cou'd leave her handsomly—and betake your self to other Women.

CARELESS
To other Women? what to do? to empty my Bones? I have had enough of variety.

WATT
Ay but, Sir, you are handsom and young; I have known such in this Town, who have brought in as good a Living, as any Miss of 'em all; kept their Coaches too, with only being a little Snout Fair.

CARELESS
Damn it, I'll ne're fall so low to do the drugery of any Old Lady.

WATT
Very good! many a younger Brother wou'd leap at such preferment.

CARELESS
No I'll pursue my first Resolves, and will commit some death-deserving Crime, tho' these Cloths go to the Hangman for't, in spight to him that was my Uncle, and that ridiculous, grave, formal Nonsensical speaking Friend of his Saveall, that calls People Pe-o-p-le.

[Enter **SAVEALL**.

Mr Saveall!—Cou'd I expect this honour? how am I oblig'd to you for this Visit?
—Sir, being inform'd my Uncle was come to Town and you with him, I did presume to write to you.

SAVEALL
Send away your Servant.

CARELESS
Go, wait without.

[Exit **WATT**

SAVEALL
One Servant is not fit to be employ'd in all Offices.—It was a bold thing indeed, to write to me, considering how often I have interceded for you, and reconcil'd you to your overgrateful Uncle, therein was your good thoughts of your self.

CARELESS
The wretchedst Creature breathing! in having wearied out my best of Friends, on whom my chiefest happiness depended.

SAVEALL
No, I am not wearied, but have the same good wishes still to serve you, but cannot strive against impetuous Torrents.

CARELESS
My Uncle's then resolv'd that I shall perish. But did you speak on my behalf this time?

SAVEALL
O Sir! I have try'd him even unto his displeasure.

CARELESS
But did you mention that good deed of mine, which he once swore shou'd ever be remember'd?

SAVEALL
All, Sir, all; but 'twas in vain to urge your merits to him, tho' to say truth, it was a worthy Action to save him, from the inhuman Violence of Thieves and Murderers—but—

CARELESS
Watt, and I, made Four of the stoutest Rogues fly for't, that ever cry'd Stand upon the Kings high way.— After they had dismounted him, and set their Pistols to his Bosom; he crying and roaring out for Assistance, I happen'd by meer Accident to pass by, which was a miraculous chance, nay it was, when I was out of his Favour too, and had been so for six Months; and yet Nature prevail'd and I sav'd him—nay more—

SAVEALL
Fare you well, Sir, I cou'd have said all this as well as you—but—

[Offers to go.

CARELESS
Good Mr Saveall, do not leave me.

SAVEALL
Good Mr Careless, give me leave to be heard as well as to hear.

CARELESS
I cry you mercy, Sir, pray proceed.

SAVEALL
I was saying what you did then for your Uncle was a worthy Action, and you exprest your self a perfectly kind Nephew; the Action too drew blessings on your head, notwithstanding you were then cast off to Reprobation, he then receiv'd you into his Bosome again, Adopted you his Son, tho but his Sisters Son, allow'd you Three hundred Pounds a year, and gave Walter Fifty Pounds for the good Service he then did.

CARELESS
And he deserv'd it, I'll say that, he receiv'd a slash over the Coxcomb, he never bore his drink well since.

SAVEALL
God be with you the second time.

CARELESS
Nay sweet Mr. Saveall—

SAVEALL
I came not altogether to hear you speak, but to speak unto you my self.

CARELESS
Sir, I will attend with all due submission.

SAVEALL
As I was saying—Sir Oliver being thus gracious unto you, you presumed upon your Merit still, and flew to new extravagancies, till for one good service you did him, he repaid you a hundred, by paying of Surgions Bills for Claps, Wounds, &c. Redeeming you out of Prison, till wearyed with your Extravagancies he turn'd you off for ever, nay even at that time—

CARELESS
Even at that time I could have liv'd, and might do so still, only by being imagin'd his Heir, had he not been Marryed: a Curse upon that Marriage, it turn'd the hearts of all well minded Citizens from me.

SAVEALL
A Third time I will take my leave.

CARELESS
Sir, You shall see the last of me first and that immediately, that you may let my Uncle know, I'll be no more a Vexation to him, unless in Charity he will see me buried; 'tis all I ask.

[Draws his Sword. **SAVEALL** gets it from him.

SAVEALL
I hope you will not kill your self and thereby damn your Soul.

CARELESS
O Sir, you need not disarm me, I can die without that help—I feel my heart ready to break; alas Sir, my Uncle has abandon'd me, and so have you, and then 'tis high time to dye—Watt—

[Enter **WATT**.

WATT
Your pleasure, Sir.

SAVEALL [Aside]
I have delay'd too long to tell him the good News I bring him.

CARELESS
Put me to Bed, Watt

[**WATT** holds him he stands as fainting.

WATT [Aside to **CARELESS**]
Mrs. Phebe is come indeed, but I hope you will not go to Bed with her before him.

CARELESS
Put me to Bed, I say—come undress me quickly.

WATT
Lord, Lord, Sir, how his heart pants! pangs of death I fear.

SAVEALL
Alas! I hope not so, good Mr. Walter. I will now be brief—Mr. Careless, pray look up.

CARELESS
No, no, Sir, I am well prepar'd to die, I thank my Stars.

SAVEALL
Why Sir Oliver is Friends with you!

CARELESS
Alas, alas Sir,—

SAVEALL
Why I thought you a Man of more resolution.

CARELESS
Ay, Ay Sir, I have made a resolution.

SAVEALL
Come Sir, I profess, all that I have done was only to search your temper.

WATT
Ay, Ay, Sir, but I am afraid you have searcht too deep.

CARELESS
Ay, Ay,—

SAVEALL
Come Sir, look up, Sir Oliver intends to take you into Grace again, and make a farther Tryal of you—you may be yet his Heir, for your New young Aunt is now out of hopes of a Child, having been Marryed at least 20 Months, and no signs of Issue.

CARELESS
Ah Sir,—can this be possible?

SAVEALL
Most possible. Come Sir, you must along with me to your Uncle; and all things shall be well again.

CARELESS

Your Generosity has reviv'd me, Sir,—Watt, my Sword.—tell Phebe I am now in haste, going to see my Uncle, and cannot stay to speak with her.

[Gives him his Sword.

SAVEALL
Good Gentleman, how feebly he stands! but his Uncles kind Aspect will recover him.

CARELESS
Sir, what if I shou'd first (to shew the Reformation of my mind) leave off my unbecoming Perriwig, and put off these gay Cloths, and Equip my self in a Students Gown? I can be furnisht at the Brokers, Sir.

SAVEALL
The Reformation of your mind's sufficient; and these Cloths become your Quality.

[Exit **SAVEALL** and **CARELESS**.

[Enter **PHEBE** to **WATT**.

PHEBE
What? he is departed, it seems.

WATT
Call'd by his happy Fortune.

PHEBE
Refuse to see me? but I'll fetch him back.

[Offers to go.

WATT
Hold, hold, sweet Phebe, you will not ruine him; he's gone to be Friends with his Uncle, and I dare promise you within a day or two, a New Gown and Petticoat.

PHEBE
You know how to dissemble too—pray let him make me amends for the wrongs he has done me, for I neither can nor will any longer bear with him.

WATT
Nor bear him neither? You had best have a care what you say.

PHEBE
Nor with him neither, Sawcebox, unless he Marry me, as he promis'd, and save my honour.

WATT
Your honour, with a Pox!

PHEBE

Yes, Sirrah, my honour, which was unspotted before he seduc'd me, which e're long I'll make him know—nay and thou shalt assist me in it.

WATT
Why look you, Mrs. Phebe, be not so passionate, and I'll do all I can to serve you.

PHEBE
'Tis your safest way, or I'll be the death of you.

WATT
Bless me, how desperate Poverty makes a Whore!—but what Course do you intend to take with him?

PHEBE
Why I intend to send my wealthy Kinsman that lives in the City to demand satisfaction of him, which if he refuses, I don't doubt but he'll hamper him.

WATT
What I'll warrant you, you mean Saleware, he that has the flanting Wife?

PHEBE
Why how now Impudence! do you mock my misery?—I'll make him know what it is to abuse simple Innocence. He had no way to accomplish his wicked design, but by promising to Marry me, and at the same time made me refuse the offers of a good match in the Country, by which I incurr'd the displeasure of all my Friends; and does he think to leave me now at last, without making some provision for me? but he shall find that my Kinsman has mony, and will stretch his purse to right me by Law.—for I have already given him an Account of his ill usage to me.

WATT
But I hope you have not told him how often he has enjoy'd you, and the Wheres, and the Whens.

PHEBE
Sirrah, I shall teach you and your Master too, to use me with more Civility ere it be long.

WATT
Why truly, Mrs. Phebe, for all my Fooling I have a perfect sense of the injuries he has done you, and have not been wanting in my perswasions to make him less cruel;—but I'll warrant you will refuse me a kiss now for all the good Offices I have done you.

[She strikes him.

PHEBE
Away you impudent Rascal.

WATT
Come prethee tempt me no farther, for if you do, by Heaven I shall be most desperately in Love with you.

PHEBE

You in Love with me, you pittiful Creature!

WATT
Yes, faith Madam, I am your Creature as well as my Masters, and can satisfie my appetite very well upon a dish after he has done with it, and you know the Servingman is always allow'd to break his Fast upon his Masters leavings—Oh, how Devillish hungry that frown makes me.

PHEBE
You are no Impudent Rascal you?

WATT
Come, come, you know a good stomach needs no sawce, and you may save your self the charge and trouble of going to Law, nor shall you need the assistance of any other Friend, to make my Master do you reason, but your Friend and Servant honest Watt—

PHEBE
In good time.

WATT
Come take my Counsel, and if I do not handle matters so (if you'll but joyn with me) as shall content you, then say I'm a Man of no Abilities.

PHEBE
How joyn with you?

WATT
In the next Room I'll shew you; there I'll dictate a Letter, which you shall write too him, which shall sting him to the quick.

PHEBE
Nay I intended to write to him before I departed the house—Oh Cozin, are you come?

[Enter **TOM SALEWARE**, as they are going off.

WATT
The Devil take this sniveling Cuckold for spoiling our sport.—hark ye, Mrs. Phebe, is this your Worshipful Kinsman you told me of.

TOM
I am the Gentleman, Sir, if you have any thing to say to me—my Kinswoman has told me all, and so pray tell your Master, and that he's a dishonest Gentleman if he does not Marry her according to his promise; 'tis that I came to demand in her right, or to denounce the Law against him.

WATT
'Twas well, Sir, that you came too late to tell him so, for he wou'd have so swinged you else—

TOM

Oh, oh, Sir, these great Speeches cannot fright me, I neither fear, nor care for swinging, I'll not be dasht, nor basht, nor cross him out of my Book for such payments; for, Sir, take notice he is in my Books for Sixscore pounds, as you can witness, tho you have lost the remembrance of me;—but Sapientia mea mihi; Stultitia tua tibi.

WATT
Oh your Servant, sweet Mr. Saleware, I had indeed forgot you—how does Mrs. Saleware, your most beautiful Wife? the Flower de Luce of Pater Noster Row.

TOM
No matter to you, Sir, how my Wife does; 'tis, my Kinswoman that I talk of, whom your Master has deflowr'd, and deluded, and led into a Fools Paradise, as the saying is, by swearing he wou'd make her his Wife, and here he has held her off, and held her on, till she is with Child by him, and I'll have you to know, Sirrah, my Cozin is a Gentlewoman.

WATT
Pray, Sir, how many Children have you, by your most exquisite Wife?

TOM
Why what's that to you? again Sirrah—still medling with my Wife?

WATT
I only spoke it, because you were talking of Children, Sir,—but how shall I know this is my Masters Child, if she has conceiv'd?

TOM
I shall make him know 'tis his. Come, come, there's Law to be had for money, money to be had for Friends, Friends to be had in the Spiritual Court; and so, if you please, you may tell your Master. Come, Cozin, come.

WATT
But pray, Sir, give me leave to ask you one question: From whom doth your Cozin derive her Gentility? Is it from you or your Wife?

TOM
Sirrah, you are a sawcy Jackanapes, to offer to meddle with your betters; for I'll have you to know, I am a Common Council Man, and as for my Wife, let me advise you not to mention her but with respect, or I shall bring you, where you shall be taught to mend your manners.

WATT
I cry you mercy, Sir, I know she's for great Persons.

TOM
Are you at it again? Well, Sirrah, remember this.—Come away, Cozin.

[Exeunt.

SCENE II

Enter **SIR OLIVER THRIVEWELL** and **LADY**.

SIR OLIVER
Why shou'd you harbour so ill an opinion of me?

LADY
Your late unkindness is too visible; did you not take me in your Arms last night, with exstasie? And when you discover'd that 'twas I, you coldly turn'd away, as if you had dreamt the while.

SIR OLIVER
Methinks you dream now, or else you cou'd not talk so idlely.

LADY
This will not do, for I'm resolv'd, I'll never let you rest, till I know what 'tis has caus'd this Melancholy.—I am sure, be it what it will, it has been but very lately entertain'd.—Come be free with me, have you enter'd into Bonds for Friends, and are forc'd to satisfy 'em?

SIR OLIVER
No, no, prethee give o're.

LADY
Or has any sad distaster befallen some dear Friend of yours?

SIR OLIVER
Fie, fie.

LADY
Or is it your extravagant Nephews wicked Courses that afflicts you?—I was in hopes you had been Friends with him, you made your Friend Mr. Saveall and I believe so. You said you wou'd send for him; have you not? or do you repent the promise which you made us?

SIR OLIVER
Neither, upon my life; when e're he comes, he shall be wellcome to me, prethee leave to be Inquisitive.

LADY
Indeed I shall not, Sir, till I know:

SIR OLIVER
Nay good wife—

LADY
No persuasion shall prevail, I will know't tho it be a sin against my self: and Ile forgive it too.

SIR OLIVER [Aside]
Now shall I play the Fool, and tell her.

LADY
You will not tell me then?

SIR OLIVER
Yes, I will, if you will be so good as to forgive it, tho you are most concern'd to punish it:

LADY
Sir, 'tis my duty to forgive any thing, and here again, I swear I will forgive it.

SIR OLIVER
Let me confirm your mercy—and on this Altar which I have transgrest, offer new vows, of Love and Faith for ever.

[Kisses her.

LADY
Again, Sir, I forgive what ere it be.

SIR OLIVER
Ile sin no more so, yet I scarce know a man that is not guilty this way—

LADY
Dear Husband, to the business. You've lov'd a pretty Woman, Is't not so? I mean—unlawfully?—

SIR OLIVER
Your guess is right; and I expect my sentence.

LADY
Ha, ha, ha, what a Coyle was here, about a thing of nothing? Where shall you find from the Carman to the States-man, one free from such a fault?—

SIR OLIVER
And can you pardon it then?

LADY
Never fear it: tho I've been jealous ever since your last being in Town.
—But pray, how many Women—have you thus lov'd?—

SIR OLIVER
Upon my life but one.

LADY
Tell me her name; tho I fancy I suspect who 'tis already.

SIR OLIVER
Saleware my Silkmans Wife.

LADY
'Tis she I meant. Pray what price? for she's a handsome woman;

SIR OLIVER
Faith after a tedious Courtship which she withstood, with much put-on Coyness and fain'd scorn, crying I had mistook my woman, she was not of that lewd sort—and so forth, at last I offer'd her a Hundred Guinies, which soften'd her into a yielding; and then I once enjoy'd her.

LADY
I guess the time too. 'Twas last Term when you stay'd out all night, and said you'd been amongst the Wits.

SIR OLIVER
Still you guess right,—but that for which I hate this jilting Quean, is, having purchast her at such a price, I thought to have lov'd on still on the old stock. But she turn'd tail—and cry'd, Another Hundred Guinies, and you're welcome; this answer I receiv'd but yesterday.

LADY [Aside]
O unmerciful! how rich would the City be, were every kindness that their Wives granted, so return'd and pay'd! Why, twould begger the Court and Country. But here comes Mr. Saveall and Mr. Careless, I believe. Faith 'tis a handsom Gentleman—

[Enter **SAVEALL** and **CARELESS**.

SAVEALL
Sir, I have according to your desire brought home your Nephew Careless; a Penitent he is, and so I recommend him.

SIR OLIVER
George, thou art welcome, nor will I perplex thee with any upbraiding of thy past offences.

CARELESS
I humbly thank you, Sir,

SIR OLIVER
Nay, not so grave, good George: Ile have thee live with all thy wonted Spirit. Leave but thy wonted lewdness and 'tis enough.

CARELESS
Sir, they only serv'd to teach me how I ought to be, by seeing my own defermity in them, and I hope, have wrought that Effect in me which you desire—

SIR OLIVER
'Tis well sayd, and, George, thank Mr. Saveall and your Aunt too, for they were your Advocates,

CARELESS
Hah! my Aunt! how beautiful she is!
[Aside gazing on her.

SIR OLIVER
Salute her, George—

CARELESS
I dare not, Sir, approach her.

SIR OLIVER [To **SAVEALL** aside]
I like that Modesty.

SAVEALL
Nay, nay, Sir, he is transform'd from what he was.

CARELESS
Madam, the goodness you have shown me, cannot be pay'd but with that reverence and respect we pay to Heaven; for when I wou'd approach you as a Lady to whom I owe obedience as an Aunt, your bounty and your Beauty gives me Laws, and thus commands my distance.

LADY
This distance is too much. You'le be more welcome, if you approach more near.

CARELESS [Aside]
I'd rather offend in my respect, than in my obedience, and since you command it—thus take the humble boldness—Ah, she's a Heavenly creature—

[Kisses her.

SIR OLIVER
George,—come hither—take notice; George, my house here is yours, my table yours: and all my Servants to be commanded by you:—but you have Watt still?

CARELESS
Yes, Sir, a very harmless honest true hearted Fellow 'tis: as I have instructed him, he has left off swearing now, and can say Grace.

SIR OLIVER
'Tis well. Send for him to wait on you: to morrow Ile pay your debts if you owe any thing.

CARELESS
Some few, Sir, hardly worth taking notice of: they shall not be your trouble—

SAVEALL
You speak well, Sir.

SIR OLIVER
Well, George, what ere they be, they shall be pay'd. Come lead your Aunt in to Dinner—

[Exeunt.

ACT SECOND

SCENE I

Saleware's Shop.

Discovers **ALITIA SALEWARE**: a **PRENTICE**, the **LADY THRIVEWELL**, and a **FOOTMAN**.

ALITIA
I assure your Ladyship, there cannot be better ware in London, and your Ladyship will find it such in the wearing.

LADY
Have you made a Bill Mrs. Saleware? for I am satisfied in the goodness of your Commodity;—a Note of the particulars I pray: and at as low a Rate as you can afford for ready money; for I am never in the City Books, like Heirs under age and Courtiers:

ALITIA
Your Ladyships pay was ever good, and I have made the Prices according. Here 'tis, Madam—

LADY
Let me see—Boy, take you the Box, 'tis all put up.

ALITIA
Yes, Madam.

LADY
Give me my Purse, Boy, and go you home with the Lace. I have only Gold, Mrs. Saleware, which you will weigh before you take, I suppose.

[Exit **BOY**.

ALITIA
That's no great pains, Madam.

LADY
How ever Ile not give you the trouble now,—pray send your man for a Glass of beer—

ALITIA [To her **BOY**]
Some beer for my Lady—

[Exit **BOY**.

LADY

That I may take the opportunity to tell you, what possibly you wou'd be loth he should hear:—for 'tis more the business of the Fore-man of the Shop to keep his Mistresses secrets.

ALITIA
Your Ladyship is merry.

LADY
Not very merry, because I find by your Bill here that I have laid out more mony than my Husband allow'd me: here is a Hundred and Eight Pounds and Two shillings, and I am allow'd but the Hundred.

ALITIA
The rest is no great matter, Madam,

LADY
Oh, very great in a Norfolk Ladys Pocket: and wou'd supply her Credit at Picket, and Lantraloo a whole Christmas in the Country: tho you great Gamesters of the City here, can lose and win your Hundreds, whilst 'tis so easily commanded out of the Pockets of those Country-Ladys Husbands—

ALITIA
I understand not your Ladyship.

LADY
Ile tell you then: Sir Oliver, when he was last in Town, lent you, or left with you, a Hundred Guinies, which he has given to me: now here is in the Bill one Hundred and Eight Pounds and Two Shillings, so here is Twelve shillings for you, and all is paid.

ALITIA
What mean you, Madam?

LADY
Why, have you forgot the Money my Husband lent you? 'tis strange, when 'twas to do you such a service.

ALITIA
A service, Madam!

LADY
Yes, a service; have a care you don't make me suspect that you deserv'd it from him some dishonest way.

ALITIA
Please you to drink, Madam?

[Enter **BOY** with a Glass of Beer.

LADY
After you Mrs. Saleware.

[**ALITIA** Drinks.

—This Notes right cast up, Boy?

BOY
To a Farthing, Madam.

[**LADY** Drinks.

ALITIA
I hope your Ladyship will find your self so well us'd, that you will always be pleas'd to Honour me with your Ladyships Custom

LADY
On these Terms always, Mrs. Saleware, and so, Your Servant.

ALITIA
Your Ladyships obedient.—Open the Coach for my Lady.

LADY
My Footman's there, he need not.

ALITIA
Wou'd your Coachman wou'd carry your Ladyship to the Devil.

[Enter **BELLAMY** as the **LADY** goes out, she gazes on him.

[**LADY** returns still gazing upon **BELLAMY**.

LADY [Aside]
Hark you, Mrs. Saleware.—sure 'tis the same.

ALITIA
Your command's an honour, Madam.

LADY
Do you know that Gentleman?

ALITIA
Yes, Madam, he is Gentleman to the Lord Loveless, and call'd Bellamy.

LADY
'Tis a hansom youth, I thought I had seen his Face before. I commend you for placing your Love here now: but an old Country Knight is a dangerous man; have a care of such, for likely, they have handsom Ladys of their own; adieu sweet Mrs. Saleware—

[Exit **LADY**

ALITIA
The Devil take her, how she shot Darts at Bellamy: she Loves the Beardless Boy, this chast Lady.

BELLAMY
Now, Madam, may I be heard?

ALITIA
Yes, if you please to speak.

BELLAMY
But you are frowning, Madam, why do those Eyes put on such Marks of anger, threatning a death to him, whom they have made their slave?

ALITIA
Fie upon't, what stuff's this, I am out of Humour, and this will increase it.

BELLAMY
Who durst offend you?

ALITIA
An unlucky accident that has happened to me, I have cozened my self in the Sale of a parcel of Goods, which if my Husband shou'd know, here wou'd be such a life—

BELLAMY
Hang him Mercenary fool, why shou'd he set you here to forward such mean Trade?

ALITIA
Ay, this talk pleases me.

BELLAMY
Ranking his Wife but with his Prentices,

ALITIA
'Tis very true, Mr. Bellamy: 'tis a mean thing as you say, but I have reveng'd it to day, in the mistake I have made.

BELLAMY
I hope it was not much?

ALITIA
Not much; but so much as has spoil'd a Shop-Trader of me: your Lord told me, I shou'd not be at this Servile pass long: that he wou'd take me from it, and carry me to the other End of the Town, and take me a House in the Pellmell—

BELLAMY [Aside]
He still designs it;—If I prevent him not.

ALITIA

He said I shou'd have new Cloths, too, and sent the Mercer to me with Patterns of Brocados de or: but I have heard nothing on't since.

BELLAMY
Perhaps this Letter will satisfie you.

[Gives her a Letter:

ALITIA [Reads]
—What a cursed office is this, to play the Pander for the man I love, I am well born, and but for his flattery, had still remain'd with Honour and in Virtue: but his bewitching tongue wrought on my easiness, and rob'd me of my Fame:—'twas well in this disguise I was conceal'd, my sister else had known me, and then I'd been undone: 'tis this—that keeps me too, conceal'd, from the false Loveless, who takes me for a Boy, and makes me do what even in this bold shape I am asham'd to act, to Pimp for him:—Oh heavens! that word—but I'll prevent his longer doting here; to wast his fortune and his love on one, common, ingrateful, and insensible.

ALITIA
O what a sweet Letter's here, and yet I have a kind of a mind to this Bellamy too—at Shatliens at six, good—
[Aside]
—Sir, I find my Lord is all honour.

BELLAMY
But, Madam, will you think on me that languish for you.

ALITIA
Because I am kind to your Lord, you imagin I must be so to you? but I wou'd have you to know I am none of those: I am not faln from his favor yet, or if I were, I shou'd not fall to Pages—there be more Lords.

BELLAMY
Madam, you have silenc'd me.

[Offers to go.

ALITIA
Nay, not so hasty, come back Mr. Bellamy.

PRENTICE
Can you take his mony forsooth?—d'ye hear, Sir.

ALITIA
Stay you behind the Counter, Sirrah; cannot I handle the Gentleman without you?—What, fly for my first denial?—Come, let a smile encourage you again—

BELLAMY
Oh how you bless me!—

ALITIA
—Come, come, leave off to talk like a Player, and if you have a passion for me, let me know't—Are you asham'd? that blush wou'd seem to say so—come then, whisper it in my ear—

[He whispers—

Oh strange, is that the highest price you dare venture? I cannot, Sir, afford it so: yet this—before you go—I'm sure you cannot match it.

[Kisses him.

BELLAMY
I shall forget my duty to my Lord—

ALITIA
Prithee do so, and so will I, and tell me what you wou'd have me to do with you.

BELLAMY
I wou'd intreat you—

ALITIA
Forward, Sir, without a blush.

BELLAMY
That you wou'd vouchsafe—

ALITIA
To do what, I pray?

BELLAMY
To wear this Watch by your side—and every minute think of me.

ALITIA
I could have done that without all this intreaty—is this all?

BELLAMY
No, there is something more, but when I think how fair you are, and what a blessing my Lord injoys in you—

ALITIA
Prithee no more of him: but ask me something.

BELLAMY
I dare not hope you can grant me any thing.

ALITIA
Why so?

BELLAMY
Because you love my Lord so well.

ALITIA
Perhaps not when he is present—but tell me what is it?

BELLAMY
That you'd be pleas'd—

ALITIA
I am pleas'd.

BELLAMY
To grace this Ring with your fair hand.

ALITIA
And what hurt will that be to your Lord?—come, come, I must divine your meaning now, and what returns I must make you for all these presents—but—

BELLAMY
But—you'll be cruel and betray me to my Lord.

ALITIA
But I will not, tho' I have you at my mercy; for it is evident you wou'd lye with me—deny it if you can.

BELLAMY
Did I name such a word now? I swear you make me blush.

ALITIA
Then you're a fool; come, take courage, and be more a man, for you shall—

BELLAMY
What shall I?

ALITIA
Why you shall—you understand me, do what I said you wish't to do.

BELLAMY
Oh how happy you will make me!

ALITIA
But 'tis on this condition.

BELLAMY
Let it be what it will I'll do't.

ALITIA
Why you saw here e'n now, a young Lady.

BELLAMY
What of her?

ALITIA
'Tis my Lady Thrivewell.

BELLAMY
Wife to Sir Oliver Thrivewell?

ALITIA
Yes; it seems you know her then.

BELLAMY
I have seen her, I think, when she was a Maid.

ALITIA
Well, she's passionately in love with you—you saw her speak to me, and how unwilling she was to go, and lose the pleasure of looking on you.

BELLAMY
What does all this tend to?

ALITIA
Nay, I speak against my self, to oblige that sweet person, which few women do; but I have particular reason for't, and you must make love to her. You know what I mean.

BELLAMY
Alass, how shou'd I get access?

ALITIA
O, my Lord's to borrow mony of her husband, and you're to be employ'd, I know upon the Message, then you'l have opportunity, and she being willing, the bus'ness may soon be done:—and 'tis the only way to win my love.

BELLAMY
This is to try my constancy.

ALITIA
I vow I do not, but will be yours intirely, when this is done;—but see my husband:—We must sup to night at Shaltines.

[Enter **TOM SALEWARE**.

TOM
How does my dear **ALITIA**?—Mr. Bellamy, your servant, I hope my Honour'd Lord's well. Why what, you are not brisk and gay! I hope my wife has not couzen'd you in any Wares; or are you and she upon some

bargain, that you cannot agree about? You must comply with Mr. Bellamy, my sweet Aly. he is my Noble Lord's Favorite, and must be us'd well, and shall, whether I am within or without doors.

BELLAMY
Sir you mistake, and I must take my leave.

[Exit **BELLAMY**

TOM
What an Asenego's this? he might a return'd my Complement, tho' I care not a fart for him. I hope thou hast couzen'd him indeed, Alitia.

ALITIA
Thomas, you are mistaken, Thomas,—in setting me to couzen any body; I am weary of this sneaking Trade, Thomas, and of this taudrum City dress, Thomas, as I have often told you, Thomas; but you think a wife shou'd obey her husband.

TOM
Never the sooner for a hasty word, sweet heart; but for these Tawdrums, as you call them, I say, they are the City-fashion: yet you may follow your own humor, and my Lord's fancy, as I promis'd before I had you.

ALITIA
Why, that's well said, Friend.

TOM
Nay, now I am sure she's pleas'd, she calls me Friend, she ever did so when she was in good humor. —But, Friend, I have found a chapman for the Lace my Lord Lack-Land bespoke, and wanted mony to pay for: a chapman that will buy it all.

ALITIA
I have sold it, Friend, already.

TOM
How, Friend, and is't paid for?

ALITIA
Yes, tis paid for.

TOM
Well, it comes as pat to stop a Gap.

ALITIA
It has stopt a gap already. I have bought me things I wanted, fine Clothes, and Tours, and Points and Knots, and—

TOM
And—never the sooner for a hasty word.

ALITIA
'Tis so, Friend, what City-Wife can draw in Customers to her Shop, that is not Lady-like? and therefore I have done it.

TOM
Say you so, say you so?—

ALITIA
What are you angry at it?

TOM
I were a beast if I should—no, no, Friend, I am not angry: let it go—& sapientia mea mihi, is my Motto.

ALITIA
Well Thomas, look to your Shop, for I must go abroad.

TOM
Pray whither?

ALITIA
How, dare you ask that question?

TOM
I am Corrected. Sam, wash your Face, and get your Cloke and Gloves and wait on your Mistriss.

ALITIA
I'le have no Sam, to tell you all he sees: In good time, is that friendly?—

TOM
I am again Corrected, but you'l return by supper time?

ALITIA
Again are you at it?

TOM
I've don, I've don.

ALITIA
I'l neither come to supper, nor to bed, perhaps.

TOM
Never the sooner for a hasty word, I hope.

ALITIA
Nor when I do come home, you shall not ask me, Where I have been, what I have done, or what Company I had?

TOM
No, no; sapientia mea mihi, I say still.

[Exeunt, **SEVERALLY**.

SCENE II

Careless his Chamber.

Enter **CARELESS**: **WATT** with a Candle.

CARELESS
Are not we in another world, Watt? And have not I improv'd my time well, already, look you here, sirrah?

[Shews Gold.

WATT
—'Tis a comfortable sight, Sir, may it long continue so.

CARELESS
I'll score no more Reckonings in Taverns now, nor hide my self in Priviledged places, to prevent the Alarms of damnable Duns, that besiege a Chamber-door as soon as day. I owe nothing now, Boy, and here's delicious Gold, besides, substantial Mettal—hark, how it rings.—

WATT
Yes, 'twill ring the Changes shortly.

CARELESS
So let it, Watt, for necessaries—and chime all out too, for I can manage my Unkle now, and drain new showrs when this is gone.

WATT
And do you call Claret, Whores, Hectors, and Fidlers, Necessaries?

CARELESS
Why yes, or the devil's in't.

WATT
What, Sir, shall go for Pious Uses, for you'l have little left?

CARELESS
Pious Uses! Art mad?

WATT

No, Sir, but I call it a pious thing, to have regard in some degree to your poor whore Phebe; she'l come railing home else, and spoil all.

CARELESS
She cannot injure me, the World's my own. Do's not all the House adore me? the Servants and the Tenants call me young Master. Do's not my Unkle let Leases, take Mortgages, and let Money in my Name? And has he not taken care I shall have a thing, call'd a Wife, worth ten thousand pound? And can I fear the Clamour of a little whore, thinkest thou?—No.

WATT
'Tis very well, Sir, and I admire your luck, but most, to see the fine young Lady, your Aunt, so kind to you; Why she outdoes your Unkle that way.

CARELESS
She shall be no loser by that, I have resolv'd she shall not go un-rewarded by me.

WATT
But still, Sir, Mrs. Phebe is forgotten.

CARELESS
You are, methinks, damnable careful of Mrs. Phebe, but I have answer'd here her impudent Letter she sent me, wherein she desir'd me to marry her, a Pox upon her:—Here, carry it her, with these ten Guineys, but do not give them her, till she promise to write, nor come no more, till I think fit to send to her.

WATT
That may be long enough, for ought I know.

CARELESS
Why, faith it may be so: for I must leave off this lewd whoring life, for reasons I have.

WATT
I Sir, I shou'd like it well, if you wou'd do so, and make it your bus'ness to court the Widow in an honourable way; you were about her once, and I think not ill receiv'd; Faith, Sir, try her again.—

CARELESS
Well, well, Sir, go you about your bus'ness.—

WATT
I'm gone, Sir.—

[Exit **WATT**.

[Enter **SAVEALL**.

CARELESS
Mr. Saveall, I see you are a man of Honour, and mean to keep your word in carrying a Letter to the Widow for me—here 'tis—ready.—

[**CARELESS** is Sealing the other Letter.

SAVEALL
It is discreetly done, Mr. Careless.

[Takes the Letter.

CARELESS
Faith I have been hard imploy'd, writing News into the Country, to several persons of Quality, of how Affairs stand in Court and City: of News of State, and News of Gallantry, all, all that has come within my knowledge.

SAVEALL
A handsome and commendable Imployment, and will improve your knowledge, and in time you may become a Parliament-man, and assist in the great Affair of the Rule of the Nation.

CARELESS
When I am married, Sir, I shall take up.

SAVEALL
I shall be over joy'd to see such good effects of my negotiation of this bus'ness.

CARELESS
Faith, Sir, I am unus'd to write to Ladys, and a little awkard in such matters, but I shall mend with practice. In the mean time I beseech you, Sir, to beg my pardon for the roughness of the Language.

SAVEALL
To the most Incomparable, and most Virtuous
[Reads]
—of her Sex, Mrs. Crosstil, present.—The outside is handsome, and promiseth the in-side to be courtly and civil.

CARELESS
Pray Heaven she have the same opinion of it: which with your kind interpretation may do much.

SAVEALL
I shall not be wanting to say all things to your advantage, and doubt not but I shall prevail in your behalf.

CARELESS
Oh, Sir, how you continue your goodness!

SAVEALL
Well, Sir, expect me and your Fortune modestly early in the morning.

CARELESS

Your Servant, Sir. Now the Devil take me if can wish him good luck, only ten thousand pound is a most delicious sum:—But who comes here? my Aunts Governant? how very like a Bawd she wou'd look in any other place? but being an Attendant on my Aunt—I may be mistaken.

[Enter **CLOSETT** with a Candle.

CLOSETT
Not to interrupt your Cogitations, Sir, I have here from my Lady brought you.—

CARELESS
What dear Closett, any thing from her is precious—

CLOSETT
A Caudle, Sir, the same her Ladyship eats to strengthen her. O, 'tis a most profitable Cordial Restorative; I made it, Sir, my self.

[He takes the Pot, and eats as he talks.

CARELESS
How am I oblig'd to her Generosity, which so far exceeds my merits!
How she graces me in all companies, and conversation, with her particular Favors: recommending me, and commending me to all the Ladys that pay her visits: Then what a care she takes of my Lodging, my Chamber, Furniture, my Table drest up, my fine Twilights, my Perfumes, and my Plate: and what not?— Why here are rich things in this Caudle too.—

CLOSETT
Have you perceiv'd that? Ile assure you, theirs Amber Greece.—

CARELESS
Ah! Closett, what pitty 'twas this fair young Aunt of mine was not married to a young man?

CLOSETT
Alas, Sir! Aye, great pitty.

CARELESS
She is the Charmingst Lady!

CLOSETT
Indeed she is so, Sir, I have known her, and serv'd her from a Child, and then she was a Charming Child: And as she grew towards Woman she was a Charming Maid. And now she is a charming Lady, as you say, Sir: And cou'd I live to see a Child of hers, I shou'd think I had liv'd long enough, unless I might live to see that have Children too: which I cou'd wish withal my heart.

CARELESS
I had rather see you at the Devil, and your Charming Lady too; but I hope my Uncles Impotence; or her honesty, will preserve her from my curse.

CLOSETT

—But, alas Sir, I shall never see her have one—

CARELESS
That's excellent.

CLOSETT
Say you so, Sir,—because 'twill hinder your being Heir? But, I thought you had valu'd your Aunt above all that.

CARELESS
So I do, Closett, I spoke of the bottom of the Caudle: that that was Excellent;

[Sups it up: She takes the Pot.

—But, dost think there are no ways, Closett, to get my Aunt with Child?

CLOSETT
Ways? Yes, yes, Sir, there are ways enow, did not her too nice Virtue spoil all.

CARELESS
Canst not thou perswade her to her good?

CLOSETT
How, Sir?

CARELESS
Nay, do not mistake me, Closett,—By this good Guiney, I meant no harm,—

CLOSETT
No, in my Conscience, Sir, yon spoke in pure Love to your Aunt.

CARELESS
—Nay,—nay,—Nay, you shall take it, Nor do I care if thou tell'st my Aunt, how dearly I love her, and how well I wish her: Nay, Gad and she were not my Aunt, tell her, I had rather get her a Son and Heir, than inherit all my Uncles Estate my self.

CLOSETT
Good heart! how passionately, and honestly he speaks! Well, 'tis a good thing to be grateful.

LADY [Calls within]
Closett, Closett.—

CLOSETT
Alas! that's my Lady calls.

CARELESS
Kiss her dear hands from me,—and tell her—oh, tell her, that—I know not what, I love her so, I cannot express it.

CLOSETT
I had forgot her message to you, I have the dullest brain of my own—

CARELESS
What was't?

CLOSETT
My Lady intreats you wou'd—

CARELESS
That I wou'd?—with all my Soul, I wou'd—

CLOSETT
My Lady, desires you—

CARELESS
Thy Lady desires me? By Heaven, and she shall have me.

CLOSETT
Lord, Sir, she desires you,—

CARELESS
The Devil take me, if I do not desire her too, for all she's wife to my Uncle.

CLOSETT
Will you not hear me out, Sir? she desires you to go abroad with her.

CARELESS
Oh, any whither, to Chelsey,—Knights-Bridge,—Branford,—Geernwich, I know all the convenient houses at every place; and will be as secret—

CLOSETT
I do not understand you, Sir.

CARELESS [Aside]
The Pox take this tongue of mine, it will be talking in the wrong place.—

CLOSETT
Well, Sir, you'll go with my Lady, Ile tell her.

CARELESS
I will: Tell her, she shall command my life.

[Enter **LADY**.

LADY
Closett, you make good hast.

CLOSETT
Madam, I was just coming. But, Mr. Careless, was talking so affectionately of your Ladyship, and so tenderly, that methoughts, I cou'd have stay'd a whole day to have heard him.

LADY
I am oblig'd to him. But, Nephew, you must go abroad with me, to the Park, and to the Exchange; if you can leave your Study so long.

CARELESS
All the world to wait on you. My dear Aunt, I have no Business, that can or shall hinder me, from sacrificing the whole time I have to live, to your Service.

LADY
Dear George, use less Complement to me.

CARELESS
Give it a kinder name, I do beseech you.—

LADY
Come, the Coach-man waits, and we shall have no time between this and Supper. You must not talk now, good Nephew.

CARELESS
I'm all obedience Madam,—but a Pox on't, I must meet my Gang at the Rose to night.—

[Exit **CARELESS** and **LADY**

CLOSETT
O that Heaven had sent my Lady such a Husband.

ACT THIRD

SCENE I

A Hall.

Discovers old **SIM** the Butler asleep in a Chair, a Candle burning almost out. After a great Noise of calling Sons of Whores, &c. and bouncing at the Door, Enter **CARELESS** drunk, all loose, and without his Perriwig.

CARELESS
Money, ye Sons of Whores? ask me for money? As if, George Careless ever paid Coach, or Chair Men—unmerciful Villains—money—no, no! This is not an Age of Payment.

SINGS.

A Pox of the cautious Fool,
That limits his time, and his Glass:
Who drinks, and who Wenches by rule,
Is Damn'd for a Cynical Ass.
But give me the Boy that is gay,
Whose time is his slave, and will drink
Beyond the dull limits of day,
And ne'r from his Company shrink.

—Who's yonder?—Old Sim—my Uncles Butler?—a—very honest—Fellow,—now is he diligently sleeping for my coming home, and most carefully—and kindly left the Door open for me:—So, ho, ho,—Old Simon,—so, ho, ho,—up, up, dull Mortal.

[Hollows in his Ear: he rowses.

I have use for thee.—Lord,! Lord!—what Sots and Beasts, some Men make of themselves, to sleep away half that short life Heaven has given them!—What will this wicked World come too?—Why Sim, ye drowsie Slave, up I say,—

[He rises and yawns.

SIM
Au, Au.—

CARELESS
Why, Sim, ye Son of a Whore, is this a time to sleep in? Open thine Eyes,—behold me, and guess what Business I have for thee.

SIM
Au, au,—anon, Sir.

CARELESS
Nay now, good Sim, now.—

SIM
Shall I never sleep more?

CARELESS
Unconscionable Simon, no reason in thy Sleep?—Come hither, Sim,—I have honest—lawful business for thee,—prithee—fetch me a Whore.—

SIM
'Tis my young Master George's voice, Au,—au,—deliver me well out of this lewd Town again, that I may have my fill of Sleep, and Pudding. Au, au,—mercy on me, who's here? Aye, 'tis he, my young Master George, at this late hour.

CARELESS
You lie, Sim, you lie,—'tis early—

SIM
So it should be, by my blinking Candle.—But how, Sir, came you in this lamentable pickle?

CARELESS
How do you mean, Sir?—

SIM
Why, Sir, wheres your Sword, and Periwincle?—sure you have been Fighting, Sir.

CARELESS
Only kickt a Couple of Chair-men—that, had the impupudence (wou'dst thou think it, Sim,) to ask me money.

SIM
Alas, Sir, that they shou'd offer it—

CARELESS
I, to me. Sim!—me that always bilk the Slaves.—

[Enter **CHAIR-MEN**, with Sword and Perriwig.

SIM
The Constable and Watch! well, a my Conscience he never came home in's life but 'twas thus attended.

CARELESS
These,—these,—are the Sons of Whores, that had the Impudence to ask me money.

1ST CHAIR-MAN
Your Worship was mistaken, we scorn to ask your Worship money, we know you better then lo, as they say,—But,—if your Worship wou'd be pleas'd to give us something to drink your Worships health, after our cold sitting up all Night, we shou'd be bound to your Worship.

CARELESS
Alas, poor Devils! Sim, give 'em a Guiney to drink. But no paying, good Sim, 'tis an ill Precedent.—

2ND CHAIR-MEN
Good Mr. Simon, consider us, for we have waited all night at the Rose Door; and he fearing only that we wou'd ask him money, fell on us, and beat us, we disarm'd him, and then to Cuffs we went: I protest, Sir, no Fault of ours.

SIM
Well, get you gone: and come again anon, and you shall be paid.

CHAIR-MEN
God bless your Worship.

[Exit **CHAIR-MEN**.

SIM
Come, Sir, will you not please to go to Bed?—'tis broad day light, and you'll wake your Uncle, and you know that may be fatal to you.

CARELESS
My Uncle! Damn my Uncle.—Sim, I tell thee in private, my Uncle's an old Cuckold; dost hear? a Cuckold, Simon.—

SIM
God forbid, Sir, my Lady's a Virtuous Lady, tho I say't.

CARELESS
Why so she is too, Sim,—but I speak of my Uncle—I say,—and I say, again—he is a Cuc-Cuckold,—or shall be a Cuckold before I have done, Sim,—my conscience urges me to't.—'twill be a work of great Humility, and Charity, and this is a wicked world, Sim,—a very wicked world; and 'tis time some should mend for Example,—and now we talk of mending, Sim,—fetch me a Whore.—

SIM
A Whore, Sir?—

CARELESS
I, Sim, a Whore.—

SIM
Bless me, Sir! Why we have none i'th'house, nor can fetch any out of Doors.

CARELESS
Sim, you lie,—Sim,—do not give your mind to lying, 'twill spoil thee,—no Whores i'th'house,—why where's Mrs. Figit, my Ladies woman? Doll the Chamber-maid? Starcht Susan, of the Landry? or greasie Bess, that's under the Cook? Or my Ladies Nurse, old Winter?—Or where's my Lady her self? she'l serve now.—No Whores i'th'house!

SIM
Deliver me! What do you mean, Sir?

CARELESS
What all sober discreet persons shou'd mean, to know all the she-things in the house,—therefore, Sirrah, fetch me a Whore; or I shall untile,—I shall.—

[Reels about with a noise.

SIM
O hold, Sir, I wou'd not for the world you shou'd be heard.

[Enter **BESS** the Scullery-maid passing by.

CARELESS

Hold! hold! there's a Female,—come hither, Wench,—come hither,—I say.—Why you drunken Baggage, can't you stand still?

SIM
Pox on you, he cou'd no sooner ask for a Whore, but you must bolt out.—

BESS
I was going to clean up my Kitchen.—

CARELESS
Hang thy Kitchen, thou must along with me, I have need of thee.—

BESS
Any service that I can do that's honest, Sir.—

CARELESS
Honest, I, I, we'll be very honest,—thou shalt only go to Bed with me a little; dear Bess, let me kiss thee.

[Kisses.

Well, 'tis a rare Wench! she wou'd victual a whole Camp; a kiss a day to each man, were a plentiful meal, she smells so of Beef and Mutton: and I have a raw stomach, and cou'd digest her now finely. Come honest Bess, let's up.—

BESS
I hope you do not take me for a Whore, Mr. George?

CARELESS
A Whore,—why what wou'd you be taken for, a Cherubin?—Can I take thee for a Nobler Creature?

BESS
Ah, fie upon you, Mr. George, I did not think you had the Face to seduce a young thing as I am.—Well, my Lady shall know't.

CARELESS
Come away, I say,—come,—you do not know what I design you, when my Nuncle dies.—

BESS
I, when will that be, trow?

CARELESS
Canst not thou put a little ingredient into his Potage?—That will do his business, and send him to Heaven without the help of a Doctor,—and then—

BESS
And what then?

CARELESS

Then, Ile marry thee, by this hand, marry thee.—Come away, and do not stand in thy own light.

SIM
Tell him you'l come, you Slut.

BESS
Well, Sir, you have overcome me; go you to bed, and I'll but pull off my Shoes, and steal up to you presently.

CARELESS
Sim, will she keep her word?

SIM
I, I warrant you, Sir; we have all found her a kind soul, and honest in that point, tho' I say't. Pray go to bed.

CARELESS
Give me some wine first.—

SIM
Wine, Sir? you have had Wine enough of all conscience, a vast quantity of Wine, a vast quantity.

CARELESS
What thou takest me to be drunk now, I'll warrant, dost thou? No, Sim, I have that rare quality,—the more I drink the soberer I am, 'tis a Miracle to me now that,—therefore give me some Wine, to set me right, that I may look thus—gravely on my Uncle.

SIM
Nay, pray, Sir, go to Bed,—

CARELESS
Dam me, Sim, I'll have your Leathern Ears, if I have no wine. So, ho, some Wine you Rascal—some Wine.

[Bawls.

SIM
Ah, good. Sir, speak softly.

CARELESS
Softly, you Bitch?—why who do I fear? Softly!—there's softly for you,—and there's ho—

[Kicks him.

SIM
I, I, Sir, you shall not hear me cry out, for all your Kicking—for your sake.—

CARELESS
Softly, quoth a, I'll softly ye.—

[Goes to run after **SIM**, throws over the Table and Chairs.

SIM
So here's fine doings! you'l be turn'd out for this anon, and I after you for my kindness in setting up for you all night.

[Cries.

CARELESS
Now am I compassionate,—dear Sim, come kiss me,—kiss me, I say.—Why you scurvy coy Rascal, why don't you kiss me?—So dry your Eyes, and hear me sing a Song that will make thee weep afresh,—Listen with reverence.

SINGS.
There was two Cats sat on a Well,
And one Cat there fell in:
But the Cat that sate by,
Wept bitterly;
Because that Cat was t'other
Cats Cozin Germin.
But the Cat, &c.

[Exit singing.

SCENE: The Widows House.

Enter **MRS CROSTILL, SAVEALL** and **BETTY**.

MRS CROSTILL
Ha, ha, ha, I suppose you know the inside of this, Mr. Saveall?

SAVEALL
No, Madam, but I believe it passionate and Courtly, as he that sent it: only indeed he commanded me to excuse the roughness of the Stile, he being unus'd to write Epistles of this Nature.

MRS CROSTILL
Ha, ha, ha. Pray Sir, read it: you must be acquainted with his excellent Stile.

SAVEALL
I am overjoy'd to see her so well pleas'd; wou'd I had brought it last night.

[Takes the Letter.

MRS CROSTILL
Read aloud, Sir, for I can never be weary of hearing it.

SAVEALL [Reads]
Thou damnable impudent Woman,—hah,—how darest thou, tho but in thy Dreams, imagin I am, or can be so great a Coxcomb as to marry thee; a sin which thou art Damn'd for but believing.—
—O Heavens! the Devil himself was sure his Secretary.

MRS CROSTILL
O Sir, proceed I pray.

SAVEALL Reads.
Dost thou not hear I am again establish't in my Uncles favor, and dost thou think I can want 5 or 10 Guinies to give a Wench, or that there are not Wenches to be found for such Sums; that I must be destined to marry you with a Pox.—

SAVEALL
I, I, 'twas the Devil that Dictated to him.

MRS CROSTILL
Pray on, Sir.

SAVEALL Reads.
No, therefore let me advise you, since you are so mad for a Husband, (tho I believe you love me, and only me,) marry a Blockhead, either in the City, or Country, that thinks there's Joys in Marriage, and I may chance to be so kind to be your Friend, by the by; and so you may have Children, like Yours, (that way,) G. Careless

MRS CROSTILL
You have not read many such Love-letters.

SAVEALL
This injury to you, Madam, is irreparable; but the affront done to me I'll fight him for.

MRS CROSTILL
Oh, Sir, he has oblig'd me beyond expression, and I beseech you tell him so: nay I'm in earnest.—For what concerns your self, do what you please.

SAVEALL
I do unsay all I said in his behalf, and beg your pardon.—

MRS CROSTILL
'Tis all one, Sir, I love him still the better; and tell him, this Letter has made such impressions here, as nothing can remove: and if you will oblige me indeed, you must bring him to me, and let me alone to speak to him, and tell him of his Letter.

SAVEALL
Sure you're not in earnest, Lady?

MRS CROSTILL

By my life, I am, and I beseech you credit me, and bring him to me to day; bring him in good humor too, and then I'l say you are my friend indeed.—

SAVEALL
I will not fail you, Lady.

[Exit **SAVEALL**.

MRS CROSTILL
Was there ever so extravagant a creature as this Careless?

BETTY
Madam, will you not be reveng'd on him?

MRS CROSTILL
Yes, Betty, the most severe way that ever woman took.—I'll love him! love him to that degree, he shall confess no hate was ever so perplexing.

BETTY
I confess, Madam, you were ever of a contradictive humour, and possibly you'l love him the better, because he has affronted you.

MRS CROSTILL
I do so, and am all impatience till I see him. Prithee give me the Song he made to me the last time he was in the Country.—

SONG.
Prithee, Widow, give o're, I cannot comply,
What shall I lie mew'd, and kept tame till I die?
A Pox of the noose, and the fools it has made,
I ne're can submit to keep up the dull trade.
In Wine and in Love, I will spend all my life,
Give me the kind Damsel, and damn the Fop-wife.
In Wine and in Love, &c.

[Exit, singing.

SCENE: The Hall again.

Enter **SIM** alone.

SIM
'Tis a meer folly to go to bed now, 'tis time to rise.—Well, Simon, well, thou art bound to give God thanks, thou wert not born a Gentleman,—some comfort that.—Mercy upon us, what lives they lead! never rise till three of the clock after noon, (or very rarely) and then they are damnable dry, and crop-sick,—but not at all hungry, so they lose both breakfast and dinner, (two great blessings;) instead of

Prayers, the first words they speak, as soon as awake, are—Damn me, how cursed drunk was I last night! Hay, Jack—some small Beer, you Vermin,—(very fine)—well—at last he gets himself dress'd, calls for his Coach (and not a word of dinner) rouls to Play-house, to that that has the bawdiest Play (for that settles his stomach,) tells as many as he meets (that he knows) how he was claw'd away last night, but forswears drinking again, for at least a day or two; then spys me a Vizard, over the benches he stalks, and there thunders a deal of leud bawdy, till he has won her heart quite; away they go, sup and get drunk in spight of vows of sobriety, and then to some convenient Mansion of pleasure, where they spew and snore away the remaining part o'th'night, and then comes repentance, and never till then have they any grace before their eyes.

[Enter **MR SAVEALL**, angry.

SAVEALL
Mr. Simon, where's your pretious young Master?

SIM
So, my pretious young Master; he has heard of his mornings revel-rout.—Sir, I know you are dissatisfi'd, as you have reason, but as you have ever been, be so good to pardon this fault too.

SAVEALL
Pardon him! I'd sooner pardon the man shou'd cuckold me. No, Sir, where is he?

SIM
Alas, Sir, you know he has not been abed above an hour or two, 'tis pity to disturb him.

SAVEALL
So, the old trade too still; I say, he must be disturbed, and that quickly too, or I shall make a foul house,—and so tell him.

SIM
Why, Lord, Mr. Saveall!—

SAVEALL
Lord me no Lords Mr. Simon, I say I will speak to him; go tell him, or I'l go to him, on such a message as shall not please him very well.

SIM
Well, Sir, I'l go, tho' it grieves my heart to wake him.

[Exit **SIM**

SAVEALL
This affront has rais'd an unusual storm in my breast, had not the Lady been of my acquaintance, and the Match of my proposing, it had never griev'd me: My comfort is, she is so humorous, that this Letter will rather bring her on, than put him off: but what she'l think of me the while—'tis for that I will be reveng'd, that I may let her see I had no hand in't.

[Enter **CARELESS** yawning, in his Night-Gown, and **SIM**.

CARELESS
Oh, Mr. Saveall—

SAVEALL
Make your self ready.

[Walking fast and angry to and fro.

CARELESS
Faith, I sat up a little late last night.—

SAVEALL
Dress you, I say.

CARELESS
Dress me, for what? 'tis too early.

SAVEALL
The better, Sir.—

CARELESS
Why do's the Widow intend to marry me instantly?

SAVEALL
No, Sir, but I intend to fight with you.

CARELESS
How, Sir?

SIM
Bless my soul, here's fine doings!

SAVEALL
What injury have I done you, that you shou'd ruin my Reputation?

CARELESS
How, Sir?

SAVEALL
You have put me on a base imployment, to carry a Letter to a Noble Lady, stuft with such Language, as your Lust, the Devil and all your Cabal of Hectors cou'd never have invented such another.

[Enter **WATT**

Cou'd not your Pimp there—serve for the base Office?

CARELESS

I do not understand you.

SAVEALL
You had better have eaten fire, or sent it with your ears, than have provok'd me thus by being the Messenger.

[Draws.

CARELESS
Forbear, and hear me, Sir, before you take a resolution to abandon me: If I must lose the Widow, by Heaven 'tis by the most unlucky mistake in the world.—Watt, come hither,—Did you carry the Letter I sent to Phebe?

WATT
Yes, Sir, and the poor soul's overjoy'd at the good News you sent her.

CARELESS
The Devil take her for a lucky whore. That Letter, Sir, was it I writ to the Widow, and that which you carried was meant for this Damsel: I know 'tis so.

SAVEALL
How cou'd it be possible you shou'd so mistake?

CARELESS
Sealing them before I had superscrib'd them, a Pox upon me: and to be charg'd with rudeness to the Widow,—when I was so religiously bent to lead a virtuous Matrimonial life.—The Letter, Sir, (for I'l confess to you) was written to a poor retaining whore of mine, whom I have turn'd off.

SAVEALL
It was not so directed.

CARELESS
No, no, Sir, there was the mistake; and Fortune's always kind to whores, those of her own trade.—Well, hang me, if 'twere not the sweetest well-pen'd thing,—Sirrah, go and fetch it back.

WATT
Lord, Sir, she'l n'ere part with it.

CARELESS
Then take it by force, you Rogue you.

WATT
What force, Sir?

CARELESS
Thus, you dog,—thus.—

[Kicks him.

This was a Plot of your's, sirrah; I believe you lye with her, you are so ready to cheat me to serve her—but I'l be reveng'd on you both.

[Kicks him.

WATT [Aside]
I, I, now we may go hang, now you are in favour with Sir Oliver—but if I do not fit you for't—

CARELESS
I am in your debt for being absent last night too, and letting Sim sit up for me, whom I abus'd.—A rogue—

[Kicks him.

WATT
'Tis all upon account, Sir.—

CARELESS
No more, Mr. Careless, 'tis sufficient and since 'twas a mischance, I am pacify'd, and will set you right with the Widow again.

CARELESS
But then she'l know of this Mistris I have had,—but the truth is, 'tis now grown so common a thing amongst the married men too, as well as the Gallants, that she cannot but forgive it, I think.—But who's here? my Aunt with a young handsom fellow; she's undrest too, Death! now am I jealous,—but for my Uncles sake,—I must needs beat him.

SAVEALL
By no means, Sir, I wou'd not have you commit such an outrage in your Aunts presence, and your Uncles house, for all the world.

CARELESS
You do not know him, Sir?

SAVEALL
Yes, Sir, I do, he is both friend and servant to a person of Honour, whom I value, the Lord Loveless.

LADY
Mr. Saveall, I must speak with you.

[They talk aside.

CARELESS
In the name of pleasure, what is this stripling imploy'd for to my Aunt? I perceive they have been in private too together, not so much as Bawd Closset to overlook 'em: 'tis a pretty youth, and I must beat it, when I see time convenient.

LADY
Mr. Saveall, pray speak to Sir Oliver, for my Lord is going to marry a rich Fortune, and will redeem his mortgaged Land that's forfeit to Sir Oliver.

SAVEALL
Six hundred pound, you say, Madam?—I will get it done for his Lordship.

CARELESS
Here's a pretty come-off! as if he were chamber'd up with her all this while to borrow mony: Ah woman, woman, what Politicks you have!

LADY
Your servant, Mr. Bellamy.

SAVEALL
I go your way, Sir, and will wait on you.

[Exit **BELLAMY** and **SAVEALL**.

CARELESS
I wou'd wait on him too.—

LADY
George, come back—whither go you?

CARELESS
To bring the young Gentleman to the gate.

LADY
Oh, you are too ceremonious, George,—tis below you.

CARELESS
So; I am instructed, Madam.—

LADY
You know not whose servant he is.

CARELESS
So, she loves him, I know it by her slighting him.—
[Aside]
Oh, Madam, there are Lords servants that may deserve the favour of Knights Ladies.

LADY
Not so, good George.

CARELESS
As the Lady may like 'em, Madam.

LADY
Sure you're not sober yet, George, or melancholy.—I hope nothing troubles you?

CARELESS
Not much, Madam.

LADY
Come, come, I know your grief, you think I am angry with you for the pickle you came home in last night, or rather this morning: but I excus'd your absence to your Uncle, pretending I had sent you to my Brother's, five mile out of Town, to do a little bus'ness for me: and you may see I am not much displeas'd by that, tho' you were with your blades, George.

CARELESS
Did you do me this good office to my Uncle?

LADY
Yes indeed, and he believ'd me.

CARELESS
Cou'd you be so good?—Indeed I was amongst 'em, but will be better temper'd for the future.

LADY
I shall be glad to see't, for your own sake.

CARELESS
I will obey your will in every thing.

LADY
Oh, had you beheld your self, and how you were hung together.

CARELESS
A drunkard is a beast, but I'l be so no more.—

LADY
That's well promis'd; and I'l reward it thus, George, there's a small stock of Gold.—

[She gives him Gold.

CARELESS
Dear Aunt, let me kiss the hand from whence such bounty flows.

LADY
Not to afflict you with all you said and did: I will only chide you for calling for whores, George.

CARELESS
Oh Lord! why did I? did I? what a wicked dog was I!

LADY

You frighted poor old Sim, with Fetch me a whore:—the poor wretch blest himself, and cry'd,—There was none i'th' house! then you roar'd out, How! no whores i'th'house? where's Figet? where starcht Susan? where's Doll, greasie Bess, or old Winter? meaning Closet, or my Lady her self?—No whores!—But why me, George, up in your Catalogue?

CARELESS
God forgive me, was I so prophane a Rogue? such an unhallow'd Rascal?

LADY
Yes, consider it well, George, and lay it to your heart, so fine, so handsome a young Gentleman to spoil himself with such lewd courses, 'tis great shame and pity.

CARELESS
A Pox on this damn'd Wine, 'tis that debauches me to all the other sins.

LADY
'Tis true, had you not been drunk, you wou'd never have medled with so sad a dirty creature, as Bess the scullion.—

CARELESS [Aside]
I, that's it she's most offended at, she's not displeas'd I call'd for her Ladyship last night; she presents me too with Gold: I will apprehend her meaning:—she wou'd have me leave off debauching, and give her a proof of my passion and my manhood.—

LADY
Come, come, be not melancholy, tho', George, for I wou'd have you still gay and pleasant, tho' not lewd.

CARELESS
Madam, you have reform'd my soul, and now I beseech you take the fruits of your good advice: I am all yours.

LADY
How mean you?

CARELESS
As I say, the most passionate Lover, the most secret Servant, that ever was blest with a Lady's favour.

LADY
Sure, Sir, you are not well?

CARELESS
Not well? Gad I defie all the Surgeons in London, that can say the contrary—I am sound, as a **BELLAMY**—

LADY
Not well in your senses, Sir.

CARELESS

Do you doubt my secresie? I'l never be drunk more to endanger my blabbing in that humour. My Uncle shall never know it.

LADY
Can you name your Uncle, and yet pursue me this shameful way?

CARELESS
Who the Devil can do you this kindness more naturally and less sinfully than my self? am I not his own flesh and blood?

LADY
Surely you do but rally?

CARELESS
By Heaven I am in earnest: try. In earnest? yes.—Come let me lead you to my chamber,—and give you the first clear proof of my intire passion.—

[Offers to pull her.

LADY
I know you can but jeast.

CARELESS
I'l convince you above.—Dear, Madam, come.

LADY
And wou'd you wrong your Uncle?

CARELESS
Why do you name him? he's not so just to you, you may Cuckold him with less sin, than lye with him; for then you are in danger, for he's a spark abroad, I can assure you.

LADY
How can you tell?

CARELESS
Oh, I have heard it every where.—But what needs all this Ceremony?—come let's up.—

LADY
Unhand me. If you provoke me, I'll undo you.—

CARELESS [Aside]
She's angry,—what a Pox, have I mistaken her?

LADY
Is this the best construction you can make of all my kindness to you?

CARELESS

Pox on't, I am not mistaken in her neither, but [Aside] apply'd my self to her, too soon after her young Monsieur had left her.—E'gad I'l tell her so too.—

LADY
Well, I see a penitence in your face, George, for what you've done; and if 'tis true, I can easily forgive you;—but here comes my woman.—

[Enter **CLOSETT**.

CARELESS
The Devil take her.

CLOSETT
Madam.—

LADY [Aside to him]
Look that you never tempt me so again.

CARELESS
Then I must dye, unless you'l yield without it.

LADY
Look handsomely, and do not betray your self, and for once you are safe.

CARELESS [Aside]
So, she'l come about again.

LADY
Well, go Cozin, and do that Affair for me I spoke of.

CARELESS
I go, Madam, I have my instructions all?

LADY
Yes, George, if you can remember.—

CARELESS
Oh, witty Devil, how she has turn'd the discourse! by which I find she puts no faith in old Maulkeena there: I love her invention.

[Exit **CARELESS**.

LADY
Now what's the news with you?

CLOSETT
A Citizen waits to speak with you, Madam.

LADY
Who is't?

CLOSETT
Mr. Saleware, Madam.

LADY
Sure his Aly has impudently told him what I have done.

CLOSETT
There's a Gentlewoman too, Madam.

LADY
Bring 'em in.

[Exit **CLOSETT**.

[Re-enters with **TOM SALEWARE** and **PHEBE**.

TOM
Madam, I humbly desire a word or two with your Ladyship, concerning my Cozen Phebe here: She's abus'd by a Gentleman that lies here, as I understand; Mr. Careless, Madam, who has damag'd her much.

LADY
Indeed!

TOM
Read this, Madam, 'twill inform you of the truth of what I say,—hold up your head, Phebe, we'll not be dasht in a good Cause.—

LADY [Reads]
Madam,
My Uncle's favour has incourag'd me to make my humble adresses to you in the way of holy Marriage, I shall not be altogether unworthy the Honour of being your Husband, since I may justly enough hope my Estate may be sutable to your desires: 'Tis long that I have had a passion for you, and impatient till I find whether 'twill be receiv'd well by you. If you vouchsafe to do so, I shall not only declare my self a good and grateful Husband, but live the happyest of all men,
Ever yours, G. Careless.
This is so far from injury, that me thinks 'tis very kind.

TOM
O but Madam, he is gone from his word, and denies this his Act and deed, like a disloyal man; and having born her in hand thus long, wou'd now cast her off: Sent his man to ravish the Letter from her, but never the sooner for a hasty word, Cozin, we'll not be dasht nor basht, I'll warrant thee.

LADY [Reads]
To the fair hands of Mrs. Phebe Gimcrack.—Is that your name?

PHEBE
I am the wretched thing that owns it, Madam.

TOM
Never the sooner for a hasty word.

LADY
I will endeavour to serve you, Mr. Saleware,—if I knew how.

TOM
O Lord, Madam, you are discreet, and if your Ladyship takes this matter in hand, I doubt not but to see my Cozin happy, and a good end of the business; but if it cannot be, I shall find Friends, nor shall her Cause be starv'd for want of monies, as they say: For we will not be dasht, nor basht; Sapientia mea mihi, is my word, and so dear Madam, I have discharg'd my mind.

LADY
Well, Mr. Saleware, I'll take care of your Kinswoman, and do my best for her.

TOM
I humbly thank you, Madam. Phebe, do you mind me? Bear your self to this Noble Lady handsomly, and high, as becomes the Family you came off; She may chance do you more good than all my high talking: I pray carry it high;—or,—Sapientia mea mihi, Stultitia tua tibi ; that's my Motto.

PHEBE
O doubt not me, Sir; nor my Carriage.—

LADY
Closett, take this young Woman up to your Chamber, and treat her well; I will do something for her: doubt not, Mr. Saleware.

[Exit **CLOSETT**, and **PHEBE**.

TOM
How I shall be bound to your Ladyship.

[Exit **LADY**.

—So, now will I home, and see if my Wife be come yet, or not, she has been out all day, and night too; but this I must bear, as we are Friends: for Sapientia, is my Motto.—

[Exit **TOM**.

SCENE: A Shop.

Discovers **ALITIA** in it fine, with **BELLAMY**.

BELLAMY
I see you design to kill me, you wou'd not else let me be a witness to those Joys which my Lord only reaps, and must look on and languish for, to conduct you to him; after that undress you, and lay you,—O, I dare not name where, but, wou'd I might never live to see him embrace you more.

ALITIA
Come, come, you shall not soften me so, you dissembling thing you?

BELLAMY
By all that's good, I am not, I speak truth:—O how you lay this morning wrapt in his dear embraces.—

ALITIA
Well, and did not you come from being wrapt in dear imbraces too, those of my Lady Thrivewell?—once more, let me hear the pleasing story,

BELLAMY
O if you lov'd me, as you say, you cou'd not take a pleasure in hearing what Joys I took with another?

ALITIA
Joys which you give, I can. Come let me hear how kind she was, and how well she lik'd you.

BELLAMY
So well she lik'd me, that she swore and I believ'd her, she never lik'd her Husband half so well.

ALITIA
Some other man perhaps she did.

BELLAMY
She vow'd, and I again believ'd; she never knew a man besides her Husband.—

ALITIA
And your self,—but then she was kind?

BELLAMY
Very kind.

ALITIA
And cou'd you,—when you pretended to me, cou'd you? Ah you're a cozening thing.

BELLAMY
Inspir'd with thoughts of you; I was grateful to her Ladyship, and she in requital to your kindness, for sending me, has sent you a hundred Guinies.

ALITIA
I, was she so obliging? Where be they?

BELLAMY

At my Chamber.

ALITIA
O the Subtilty of these men! for fear I shou'd not keep my assignation, yon think to oblige me that way, to come to you; but you may believe, my dear Bellamy, I am all yours, and will be so when e're you name the time.

[Enter **TOM SALEWARE**.

TOM
On my Conscience, my wife's not come home yet: Well, thus it must be, in spight of chance, and high heel Shoes which will go a wry sometimes. How a Lady there,—and my Wife not with her?—hah,—my Wife? Stay, are my Eyes mine own?—'tis she—my friend Wife, in that t'other end o'th' Town habit she has so long wisht for: but, Mr. Bellamy, and she are whispering, I must not yet advance.

BELLAMY
This night let it be.—

ALITIA
You have had enough of your Lady, sure for one day?

BELLAMY
Doubt me not, dearest, Madam?

TOM
So, Madam, is't come to that? wou'd they had done, that I might approach without interruption.

ALITIA
And with all faith and secresie, I am undone else: for you know my vows to my Lord.

BELLAMY
You undo me with these suspitions.

ALITIA
See my Husband.—Pray, Sir, present my service, and humble thanks, to my Lord, and my Husbands too.—

TOM
Yes, I beseech you, Sir.—

BELLAMY
I will obey you, Madam.—

[Exit **BELLAMY**.

TOM

—Still, I say, this is an Assenego, he will never stand a Complement with me: But, Sapientia mea mihi;—but, what new Graces has his Lordship done us, that you have made me send him thanks for? For you say, you bought these rich Cloths your self.

ALITIA
'Tis enough, I am sensible, and you may leave your silly impertinent inquisitions.

TOM
I stand corrected, Friend.

ALITIA
And stand still corrected, or I shall break the Peace with you.

TOM
Never the sooner for a hasty word.

ALITIA
Before I marry'd you, did not my Lord make you Indent with me, to ask me no Questions, to deny me nothing I had a mind too, either for wearing, or eating, or going abroad where and with whom I pleas'd; and did you not agree to all this?

TOM
I did, and will still hold to my Indentures with my Noble Lord: whose favor I wou'd not loose, for Forty Indentures.

ALITIA
O wou'd you not so.

TOM
And what the dickins care I for my spightful Neighbours, who because they cannot maintain their Wives so fine as thou art, asperse thee,—and cry there's Tom Salewares fine Wife: but Sapientia mea mihi, is my Motto; Let the Assenegoes tattle their hearts out, for I am resolv'd to show my self a dutiful Husband, in spight of Fortune and foul weather.

ALITIA
To prevent their talking, I'll remove out of their sight, and leave your pittiful Shop keeping.

TOM
Never the sooner for a hasty word.

ALITIA
Nay, I'll do't. I have been about it: have all under one done other Business too.

TOM [Aside]
I cou'd tell her under who, if I durst too.

ALITIA
What's that you mumble there, to your self?

TOM
I was only Divining what that business shou'd be, which you did all under one; Ile warrant, you have taken fine Lodgings in the Mall, as you intended.

ALITIA
No; but I have taken a house there, by my Lords directions.

TOM
How, how, what must I then break up Shop?

ALITIA
No indeed, look to your Shop, and keep your City house too, for your self to lie in.

TOM
Must I not then lie in the same house?

ALITIA
No, Friend, not unless you mean to break with me for ever.

TOM
Well,—I will not disoblige thee, nor my Noble Lord, for any Consideration, for you know my Motto; Sapientia mea mihi; Stultitia tua tibi.—And so let's in to Dinner.

[Exeunt.

ACT FOURTH

SCENE I

Enter **MRS CROSTILL**, **LORD LOVELESS** and **BELLAMY**.

LORD LOVELESS
Madam, I'm but a bashful Lover, unskill'd to court a Widow, to swear I love you,—must and will have you;—And want the moving confidence to stir your blood by putting you to't, before the Priest declare it lawful;—But, I have Love and tenderness, which you will find in all the Actions of my life.

BELLAMY [Aside]
This modest Courtship will do no good on the Widow, he has mistook her humor. Blest mistake!

MRS CROSTILL
My Lord, I am not worthy your regard, my Birth, and Education, are not sutable to your great Fame. Fortune, 'tis true, was kind and gave me wealth, which sets me up a Mark for every Man, that aims at riches: Whilst all my little Beauties lie dead upon my hands, none court for that in a Wife; 'Tis enough, his Mistris shall be fair.

LORD LOVELESS
Madam, you seem to upbraid me with a sin, I vow, I never knew,—I am so Innocent.—

MRS CROSTILL
That 'twere pitty Marriage shou'd debauch yor Lordship.

LORD LOVELESS
It cannot, Madam, I'll be so true to you,—so faithful, and so just—

MRS CROSTILL
Impossible! I wou'd not have you so degenerate from the true gallantry of your Sex, and Age, to be a constant Husband. O how vile a sound it has! a young Lord, and constant to his Wife! Not for the World, wou'd I be that Woman, that shou'd be guilty of making you so strange a Monster.

LORD LOVELESS
Madam, by my Honour, I never lov'd till now, and you may rally as you please; but, I again protest 'tis not your wealth, but Virtue I admire: and you I must possess, or be for ever wretched.

[Enter **SAVEALL** and **CARELESS**.

SAVEALL
—Stay,—let us retire again, here is the Lord Loveless.

CARELESS
Let there be the Devil, I'll not retire an Inch,—Save you, Widow.—

[Goes up to her: putting the **LORD LOVELESS** by roughly.

MRS CROSTILL
What rudeness is this?

CARELESS
Widow, I am in hast, and have not leasure for long whining Courtship.

LORD LOVELESS
Mr. Saveall, what Fellow's this, you have brought to affront me?

SAVEALL
Your Pardon, good my Lord, we knew not of your Lordships being here; 'tis Mr. Careless, Nephew to Sir Oliver Thrivewell,—of whom I have procur'd the Five hundred pound, your Lordship desir'd by Mr. Bellamy.

LORD LOVELESS
For that I thank you; but for him, I must have an account of his rudeness.

SAVEALL
Pray have respect to the presence of the Widow, my good Lord.—

LORD LOVELESS
I shall do as becomes me, Sir.

[Talks to **SAVEALL**

MRS CROSTILL
Then it seems, you do not deny the Letter, to be your own hand?

CARELESS
No, faith, Widow.

MRS CROSTILL
Have you the impudence to confess it?

CARELESS
Yes, and will not ask your Pardon for't; why what the Devil was there, that was not kind? I offer'd, if you Marry'd, to do your Drudgery, 'Egad I think you're beholden to me.

LORD LOVELESS
Madam, I made my first Addresses to you, and desire the favour of being first heard.

CARELESS
Sir, she shall hear me first, whoere came first I care not, she has heard you first already; or you have lost time.

LORD LOVELESS
Sir, I have been heard, and I will be heard again, and what's all this to you?

CARELESS
But you shall not, Sir; let me see you dare speak a Syllable to this Widow; or but tell her you love her with your Eyes, and it shall be your last; by Heaven it shall.

LORD LOVELESS
Unhand me, Saveall.—

MRS CROSTILL
How dare you, Sir, use this insolence in my house? On what incouragement, or by what Authority is it?

CARELESS
Good pert thing, hold thy prating, for let me tell thee, I neither love thee, my self, as you perhaps vainly imagin, nor will I suffer any other to do so.

MRS CROSTILL
I beseech your Lordship, to Pardon him, he's certainly mad.

CARELESS
The fitter for you, Widow.

LORD LOVELESS
Madam, the respect I bear you ties my hands, or you shou'd see I wou'd not be affronted.—Mr. Careless, you know me I suppose, and pray expect me to morrow morning.

CARELESS
I shall, Sir, I shall. You have your answer, Sir, and may be gone.

LORD LOVELESS
Death, shall my fears of angring her, make me endure all this?

MRS CROSTILL
Sir, what's your business here? what have you to say to me? If any thing, say it quickly, and leave me free.

CARELESS
Softly, good Widow, you are so impatient, till you hear me say, I love you,—well, know then I do love you most abominably, and am resolv'd to Marry you, and then to use you as I list.

MRS CROSTILL
Pray, Sir, how old are you?

CARELESS [In a whining Tone]
O parlous Wit! what, I warrant you expect to be Courted in fine Language;—Ah, cruel Woman, how can you treat a Gentleman that loves you dearer than his Eyes, so rigorously? One that cannot,—nay, will not, (whilst there are ways to dye,) live out of your favor.

MRS CROSTILL
Who is't, you speak of, Sir?—

CARELESS
I am the wretched Man.—

MRS CROSTILL [In a whining Tone too]
All this, and more, Sir, my heart directs to an unknown youth, who loves not me.

CARELESS
Death, but you shall not, Ile have you love none but me.

MRS CROSTILL
I cannot chuse, you're such a civil Person, and write such passionate stuff in your Letter.—

CARELESS
O does that Letter trouble you? In good time, Ile write more, and worse to you hereafter, and in earnest too.—Did I not tell you the mistake, unreasonable Creature?

MRS CROSTILL
Sir, I have nothing to say to you; and beg your Pardon, if I tell you, I desire you no more to visit me.

CARELESS
Why, then fare you well. Ile have as good a Widow, on every Ale-house Chimney.
[Sings. O she's a dainty Widow.

MRS CROSTILL
O how his humour pleases me, yet now Ile be reveng'd on't.—Sir, your Servant, will your Lordship please to walk in? This rude Fellow has disorder'd you?

LORD LOVELESS
Madam, you honour your servant, and fully make amens, for all I've suffer'd, in the Allowance of this favor.

[Offers to lead her in.

CARELESS
But, Sir, I am not pleas'd she shou'd allow it you.

[He pushes him away.

LORD LOVELESS
Death, Sir, But she shall.—

[Offers to draw, the rest part 'em.

MRS CROSTILL
Shall you control me, in my own house?—Pray learn to know your self.—Mr. Saveall, pray carry him away; or Ile have it done more indescently.

[Exit **LORD LOVELESS** and **WIDOW**.

CARELESS
I will endure it for once; because I know 'twas done only in revenge to me.—But who's here? My fine young dandy-prat,—and at the Widows too!—Sir, I have seen you but twice, and 'twas at places where I cannot allow of your coming, first at my Aunts, and now here at my Widows.

[Sees **BELLAMY**.

BELLAMY
Your Widow, good Sir? I thought she had been the Widow of one deceas'd?

CARELESS
Thou art a pretty witty child; but, Sirrah, let me find you here no more, nor at my Aunts, I charge you: if I do, I shall have you whip't.

BELLAMY
I hear your Charge, Sir; but you must leave it to my discretion, whether I will obey you, or not.

CARELESS

Well, Sir, remember I have given you fair warning.

SAVEALL
Sir, will it please you to walk homeward?

CARELESS
You must excuse me, Sir, at present.

SAVEALL
It will not be convenient, Sir, to visit the Widow again to day.

CARELESS
O fear it not, Sir, I do not like her so well now.

SAVEALL
Do your pleasure, Sir,—Farewell.

[Exit **SAVEALL**

CARELESS
This damn'd Widow sticks in my Stomach, I am resolv'd she shall not have me now, unless she court me to't, to which end, I will go drink her out of my head, for to my heart she is not yet arriv'd; and then Ile home, and do that which only my Aunt and I must be acquainted with: this is her Night of grace, she has promis'd me to be kind; if she keep touch with me,—O how I shall love.—

[Goes.

BELLAMY
So, they are gone.—And now must I prepare to meet Mrs. Saleware, I have a mind to try her honesty, which I believe is as little, as her faith to my Lord: I have appointed her to meet me at a certain convenient house, where I have got a Bed ready; but how to supply her with a bedfellow suitable to her humour, I cannot tell: I have therefore writ this, in an unknown name, to her Husband, who shall come and prevent the Plot, and save my credit;—but If he fail?—wou'd that were my greatest grief; but here I leave the man my soul adores, courting another, may she be deaf to all his Love, as I was to my reason, when it pleaded against his false addresses.—

[Goes out.

SCENE: The Lady Thrivewell's Chamber.

Enter **LADY**, **PHEBE**, and **CLOSETT**.

LADY
In troth, I pity you, but you were to blame too, Phebe, I must needs say, to yield.

PHEBE

'Twas the effects of Love, Madam, and his solicitations.

LADY
Well, well, I'l see what I can do for you, tho' it be but for the pleasure of revenge for attempting me:— Closet, you know my mind,—and how to order our design?

CLOSETT
Doubt me not, Madam.

LADY
I hope he will get himself fudled to night, to further it.

CLOSETT
Then he may forget your Ladyships promise.

PHEBE
No, no, then he'l be the more earnest.

LADY
You know his humor best that way, it seems,—but away, here comes Sir Oliver.—

[Exit **CLOSETT** and **PHEBE**

[Enter **SIR OLIVER**, and **WATT**.

SIR OLIVER
Make love to my wife? a fine young Rogue!—Well, Watt, for this discovery, I'l reward thee bountifully.—Sweet-heart, I have a sute to you.

LADY
Pray what is't? you may command me.

SIR OLIVER
'Tis for my absence from thee, to accompany a friend to Dover, who is going for Holland.

LADY
I hope this is no excuse to go again to your Citizen's wife.

SIR OLIVER [Aside]
Think no more of that, Sweet-heart, but expect me to morrow at dinner; if I be not here before, and catch you napping, my free Lady.

LADY
His absence falls out luckily,

[Exit **SIR OLIVER** and **WATT**.

—lest there shou'd happen any noise in the house by his unruly Nephew, in case he shou'd discover the cheat I put upon him, his own wench instead of my self. I thought I had sufficiently chid him for his rash attempting me: and he to pursue it, and urge me to a promise!—which I made to be rid of him, is what I must be reveng'd on him for.

[Enter **CLOSETT**.

CLOSETT
Your Nephew is come, Madam, and very much uppish (as they say) but not so far gon as to forget your Ladyships Promise, and he is gone to bed, in expectation of your coming.

LADY
And have you drest his Mistris up, as I directed?

CLOSETT
Oh, most famously, Madam.

LADY
But have you charg'd her to steal from him, before it is light?

CLOSETT
Yes, I have, Madam.

[Exit **LADY, CLOSETT**.

[Enter **BELLAMY**, and **TOM SALEWARE**, as in a Bawdy-house.

TOM
Why Lord, Mr. Bellamy, you are the strangest man in the World, to think I am jealous, because I ask for my Aly. I am an Asenego, if I be.—But yet I know she's here.

BELLAMY
Why look you now, is not this jealousie, not to believe me?

TOM
Oh, you equivocate, Mr. Bellamy, I protest you do; she is not indeed here at the door, but I'll warrant you she's above, but what's that to me?—Alas, Sir, it cannot make me jealous.—I hope I shall see her safe at home, some time or other, at her own leisure.—But it is a hard case tho.

BELLAMY
Now are you relapsing into your jealousie again?

TOM
What an Asenego's this? there's no man in the City more confident of his wife, than I am of my Aly: nor will I be dasht or basht at any scandalous reports that go of her, therefore tell me, whether she's here or no, for I don't come to disturb her.

BELLAMY

There, you are jealous again.—But to end all disputes, Sir, your wife is here, and I believe going to bed by this time.

TOM
Why what a notable merry Scab are you, Mr. Bellamy?—Away, away, I faith you're a Wag now.

BELLAMY
What, you will not believe me now?

TOM
Believe you? why no, by my troth, not I.

BELLAMY
What made you fancy she was here?

TOM
I fancy, Sir, I have as few fancies as any man breathing,—but I receiv'd a Note from one Mr. Spywell, hinting that my Aly was to lye with a certain Friend here all night.—A very pleasant bus'ness; as if I believ'd it:—not I, Sir, I protest, for she has no friend but my Lord, and as if he wou'd bring her to such a place as this, he having such Lodgings of his own, and she a House—is a ridiculous bus'ness.—

BELLAMY
Why did you come then?

TOM
To see the meaning of this Spywell's Letter, who bid me come and inquire for you.

BELLAMY
Well, and here I am.

TOM
Well, and what of that? he's an Asenego that inquires further: and so farewell to you.

BELLAMY
Stay, Sir, I was that Spywell that writ to you, for I knowing you had not lain with your wife this three months, out of pure kindness, laid this Plot, that you might come and lye with her here.

TOM
Why, and is she here indeed?

BELLAMY
Come along with me, and be convinc'd.

TOM
This is a Plot laid by my wife to oblige me: I am sure 'tis so. Ah little Rogue, how I will pay thy kindness!

[Exit after **BELLAMY**.

SCENE: A Bed-chamber.

ALITIA sitting in her Night-gown at a Table, undressing her. To her BELLAMY and TOM at the door.

BELLAMY
If you say I sent for you, you'l spoil all, but you must say you came by inspiration, or that you were inform'd in a dream, or a vision, or so forth.

TOM
I warrant you, Mr. Bellamy, for acting my part well. My wife has laid this Plot to give me a sure proof of her honesty.—

BELLAMY
Credulous fool!—well stand you behind this door, and I'l go in and speak to her.

TOM
Ay, ay, Sir, I'l warrant you, I'l stand close.

ALITIA
Ah, Mr. Bellamy, are you come? you are a fine man, to make me languish thus long without you, are you not?—Come, hast to undress you, and let us to bed.

TOM [Aside]
So, very good, ha, ha, ha.—

ALITIA
What does your Passion that was to day so high, decay already?

TOM [Aside]
That's pleasant again, as if I were such a fool, to think such an Asonego as he had ever had a Passion for her,—ha, ha, ha.—

ALITIA
Did you only court me to a consent to despise me for it afterwards?

TOM [Aside]
As if she had ever consented to lye with my Lord's man; a pretty bus'ness, that.

ALITIA
Or you perhaps, malitious as you are, courted me only to try me, and then betray me.—Will you not answer me?

BELLAMY
Oh Madam, I am so surpris'd with an accident that you little dream of, that I am not able to utter a word.

TOM
Was there ever such witty waggish Rogues seen as these two? what a pretty Plot have they laid to make me jealous?

ALITIA
Speak again, what is it has happen'd?

BELLAMY
Death, I cou'd find in my heart to kill the cuckoldly Idiot, the horn'd beast, for preventing my dear expectations thus.—

TOM
As I am a Christian, this is very pretty sport, ha, ha, ha.

ALITIA
What's the matter? what Cuckold, my husband?—

BELLAMY
Ay, ay, I know not by what damn'd Witchcraft, but he knows we are here; the Devil assisted him sure to find us.

ALITIA
Oh, I am ruin'd then: he'l tell all to my Lord.

TOM
Never the sooner for a hasty word.—I shou'd ruin my self then too: no, no, sapientia mea mihi, is my Motto; be not dasht or basht for that, good Friend.

[**TOM** comes out to her.

ALITIA
Hah, my husband's here indeed.

TOM
As sure as you are there, sweet Alitia. What, you thought to make me jealous now? but I thank my reason, I have more grace than so: no, I know what's what, as my Friend Hudibras has it. Make me jealous! honest Tom?—no, Mr. Bellamy, I am beholden to you.—But how I came hither, you shall never know, nor, do you hear me talk of any Letter or Porter that came to give me intelligence, no, nor name, Mr. Spywell, not I, sapientia, is my Motto.

BELLAMY [Aside]
Death! the fool will out with all.

ALITIA
What means all this?

TOM

I mean? I know what you mean; come, come, never blush for the matter, you might have told me you had a mind to.—

ALITIA
To what, Coxcomb?

TOM
Ha, ha, ha, I, I, never put on this fain'd anger, the Plot is discover'd, and I am not jealous.

ALITIA
What Plot?

TOM
That you had a mind to do me the honour of letting me lye with you to night, and now 'tis out.—Mr. Bellamy, I hope we shall have your company, tho not in the same bed, and E'faith, we'l have a Sack-Posset before we go to bed, sweet Alitia.

ALITIA
What a defeat is here!—
[Aside]
Mr. Bellamy, hark ye.—Thomas, be at a distance.

TOM
Face about, **TOM**

[Turns.

ALITIA
You have betray'd me every way: I see it plain, and will be reveng'd on you, if I live.

BELLAMY
Who, I by all.—

ALITIA
No swearing, you are a young Hypocrite: where's the hundred Guineys you had for me,—you said?

BELLAMY
And have;—but shall I give them you before your husband?

ALITIA
Come, come, I see I am abus'd and fool'd; who was it sent for him, hah?—not you, I'l warrant.

BELLAMY
Not I, I vow by your fair dear self, and am so mad, that he has defeated me, that if you'l give me leave, I'l kill him, to enjoy thee.—

ALITIA
No, hold; if this be true, I'm reconcil'd again, and pray let's meet again to morrow.

BELLAMY
May all that's man about me forsake me, if I lose any opportunity: and so I'll take my leave.—

[Offers to go.

TOM
Nay, E'faith we'l have a Sack-Posset, as I said, before we go to bed.—

ALITIA
Well, tho I seem to believe him, I am resolv'd he has done me this injury.
And when a willing woman is so crost,
All thoughts, but of revenge, are lost.

TOM
Tell me, Alitia indeed, how you came hither.

ALITIA
You will not be angry then?

TOM
I am an Asenego, if I be.

ALITIA
It was indeed to make thee jealous.

TOM
Now hang me, if I did not imagin so: nay, nay, I can prophesie right sometimes.

ALITIA
And how do you think you were brought hither?

TOM
Nay, I can prophesie that too: Mr. Spywell's Letter—but I'l say no more.

ALITIA
Ha, ha, ha, let's see the Letter.

TOM
Hah,—where is't?—hum,—have I lost it?—and facks so I have.—

[Searching for the Letter.

ALITIA
Well, well, 'twas I that sent it, Simpleton.—

TOM

Why didst thou indeed, and indeed?—Well, let's to bed, for I am now so in love with thy pretty Project, that I fancy strange things: Come, let's to bed, we'l get a Sibyl or a small Prophet this night.

[Exeunt.

SCENE: Sir Oliver's House.

Enter **PHEBE**, passing over the Stage in a Night-Gown, **CARELESS** after her, groping as in the dark, in a Night-Gown.

CARELESS
Oh stay, my dear Aunt, stay, 'tis not near day yet, we have many minutes of joy to come ere that approach.—She's gone,—I heard her Chamber door open,—wou'd I cou'd find it,—my Uncle's not at home, and I'l go to her there.—Who's this? one with lights?

[Enter **LADY** with a light, and in a Night Gown.

LADY
Is the Devil in you, that you make such a noise at this hour.

CARELESS
Wou'd it not make a man distracted to be so soon left by so sweet, so dear a Creature?—Come let's retire again.—

LADY
Sure you are mad to desire it, 'twill ruin us both.

CARELESS
I'l warrant you: my charming obliging Aunt!—

[Enter **CLOSETT**.

CLOSETT
Oh Madam, don't you hear some body knock at the door? on my conscience 'tis Sir Oliver, by the authority of clamour he makes there.

LADY
I hope not.

CARELESS
E'gad and so do I, I hope 'tis that Rogue Watt, having forgot I have turn'd him away, and is drunk. Come,—let's retire again, can we be sensible of any thing but joy?

LADY [Whispers]
Hark ye, Closet,—go.—

CLOSETT
It shall be so.

[Exit **CLOSETT**.

CARELESS
That was kind, and well thought on, to give her instructions what to do.

LADY
You cannot guess at what I said.

CARELESS
Why, to tell my Uncle, that—you are not well,—and desire him to lye by himself to night, or—

LADY
Thou art so lewd a fellow, thou canst not think one sober thought of me, which makes me now repent the favors I have done thee: be gone, and see my face no more.—

CARELESS
How unreasonable is a woman when her own turn's serv'd!—Hark ye, dear Aunt.—

LADY
Approach me not; if thou dost, I'll raise the house.

CARELESS
Unmerciful creature! do not provoke my love, which is so high, 'tis arriv'd almost to rage, do not; you know not what 'twill make me do, for now you are in my power, have a care,—I say, have a care.—

[Enter **SIR OLIVER** at the door, with **WATT** and **SAVEALL**.

LADY
Dare you do so base a thing, as to proclaim my shameful kindness? perjur'd man!

CARELESS
Why do you provoke me then, do you think to kindle a fire in my heart, and let it burn out alone? No, I am resolv'd it shall be laid.—Come, come, by all that's good, dear Aunt, I love you; and love you ten times more since you were kind, then before, and I think the Devil's in you if you desire a man shou'd do more.

LADY
I am undone.

CARELESS
Alas, that ever you were kind.—How prettily this penitence becomes you. Come, now a tear or two, and then—thou wilt be fit to be undone again.

[Enter **SIR OLIVER**, and the rest.

SIR OLIVER
Oh Monster, Villain, Rascal, what dost thou merit for this baseness, but death immediately from my hand?—And thou false woman, that hast thus betray'd me.—

CARELESS
What Devil sent him hither?

LADY
Pray hear me, Sir.

SIR OLIVER
Can I hear more to convince me thou art false, or I unhappy,—then what I've heard already?

LADY
I was not so unreasonable when Mrs. Saleware and you were kind.

SIR OLIVER
And did you, perfidious woman, pardon me that, to be reveng'd on me this way.

LADY
Mistake me not, nor wrong me: I have only show'd you what some wou'd have done.—Sir, 'twas my design, to let you see this extravagance of your Nephew.

CARELESS
O witty, dear Devil, how I love thee for thy rare quality—of dissembling.

SIR OLIVER [To **SAVEALL**]
Oh, she's the falsest woman.—

LADY
Mr. Saveall, you have ever been most obliging, pray perswade Sir Oliver to retire into my Chamber, and hear with patience what I have to say to him, he shall find there the cause of this mistake.

SAVEALL
I'l do my best to serve you, Madam.

SIR OLIVER
And dost thou think ever to reconcile me?—

SAVEALL
'Twill not be the part of a judicious man to condemn before the cause be heard, good Sir Oliver, as I take it, let me intreat that justice from you.

SIR OLIVER
Well, Madam, I will hear you, tho no false tale thou canst devise, shall perswade me against my senses. But, Sirrah, for your part—get you out of my doors, I'l see thee starve and beg, for an ungrateful reprobate, as thou art.—

LADY
Indeed you must not put him out of doors.

SIR OLIVER
How! dare you take his part?

LADY
Yes, I dare and will justifie it, nor shall you give him a word or look, that declares anger, you shall not, Sir, 'till you have heard me, and then take your course.

CARELESS [Aside]
Kind soul! I cou'd kiss her all over for this.

SIR OLIVER
You're very confident, but I'l forbear, till I've heard you, tho thou canst say nothing to make me think thou'rt innocent.

LADY
Go,—go to bed again, George, and sleep, without fear of any thing, all shall be well again.

[Exit **SIR OLIVER** and all but **CARELESS**.

CARELESS
Sweet dear charming gilt, how I love thee! now will she manage my Uncle so, that 'tis ten to one but I shall be rewarded for my nights work to morrow: but Lord, how she thought to terrifie me, with chiding me, and repenting her kindness to me. Now—go to bed, George, ha, ha, ha.—
Well go thy ways, I know thy Plots will hit:
There's nothing like a womans sudden wit.

[Exit.

ACT FIFTH

SCENE I

SCENE: The Lord's Lodgings.

Enter **LORD** and **PAGE**.

LORD
To speak with me?

PAGE
Yes, my Lord.

LORD

Bring em in.

[Exit **PAGE**, returns with **TOM SALEWARE** and **ALITIA**.

ALITIA
Pray, Thomas, attend at a distance.

TOM
Face about, Tom Saleware,—and March forwards; that I learnt at Finsbury Muster.

[**ALITIA** weeps.

LORD
How now, in tears, why is that lovely face where all my souls delight dwells, thus strangely drest in sorrow?

ALITIA
Alas, my dear Lord.—

LORD
Who is't dares injure thee? I know thy Husband is better manner'd, than to offend thee; and any other cannot escape with life.—Come name the cause.

ALITIA
There is a man has Injur'd me; but one below you, my dear Lord, to take notice of, your servant Bellamy may do't. Do you believe him honest, my dear Lord?

LORD
Most perfectly so, if I have any judgment.

ALITIA
I know, my dear Lord, you ever esteem'd him so: but,—if your Lordship had a Jewel, or any other thing, you valu'd and wou'd reserve for your own wearing, wou'd you let him enjoy it too?

LORD
I know not any thing I shou'd refuse him the use of: except, thy dear self, where I can brook no Rivals.

ALITIA
Yet he, my Lord, has wickedly attempted me, and in that has wrong'd your Honour, and your trust.

LORD
You surprize me!

ALITIA
My Lord, 'tis truth.

LORD
It cannot be. I know he durst not do't.

ALITIA
Must I not then find credit?

LORD
Give me some circumstances, but to prove it.

ALITIA
Tho if I had said it only, 'twere sufficient: yet you shall have circumstances. Thomas,—come hither Thomas. Pray tell his Lordship, what you heard and saw, last night between Mr. Bellamy, and I.

TOM
Why may't please your Lordship, my Alitia was abroad all the afternoon yesterday, as she often is, may't please your Lordship, and may as often be again, an't please your Lordship.

LORD
'Tis well,—forward.

TOM
Well, out she was, an't please your Lordship, it grew late, and no Alitia came, it grew later and no Alitia came yet, so that I e'en concluded she wou'd stay all night, an't please your Lordship, as she has done many a night, an't please your Lordship.

LORD
Prethee proceed.

TOM
I shall, an't please your Lordship. It being late, an't like your Lordship, as I said before, an't please your Lordship, I had word brought me, an't please your Lordship, that my Alitia was to lye with a Friend, an't please your Lordship, at a certain house in Drury Lane, an't please your Lordship; well, I went, and because I hate to be tedious, or hold your Lordship in a long tale, I will only say, an't please your Lordship, I went thither, as I said, and found my Alitia just undrest for Bed, Mr. Bellamy, ready to go into Bed to her.

LORD
It cannot be!

TOM
Be? why Ile justifie it, an't please your Lordship.

LORD
Then your Wife's guilty too; how came she thither?

ALITIA
I hope you will not think so ill of me, my dear Lord, alas, I was betray'd, the cunning Villain told me your Lordship was to be there, and desir'd my company; when I came and found you not, he bid me undress me, and get me to bed, and you, my dear Lord, wou'd come to me. At last I finding 'twas but a Cheat, and not knowing how to get away, writ a Note to my Husband, to come and relieve me.

LORD
Is't possible a man that weeps, and blushes, shou'd be such an one?

TOM
I vow to Gad, an't please your Lordship, I fancy'd all the while they had but play'd the wag, to make me jealous; and Alitia (ah, the little cunning Gipsie) knowing I was peeping at the door. Cry'd come to bed, Mr. Bellamy, make hast and undress you, Mr. Bellamy.

ALITIA [Aside]
Peace, Fool,—he'll spoil all.—

TOM
Mum.—

LORD
I do not like this. Where's the Letter?

TOM
Here, an't please your Lordship.—

[Gives him the Letter.

ALITIA
The Devil take you for giving him the Letter. You said you had lost it.

TOM
I thought so Friend; but I found it since.

ALITIA
Thou'dst better have swallow'd it full of Opium.

TOM
I wou'd I had so too, for me, rather than have offended thee.

LORD [Reads]
Mr. Saleware,
If you wou'd not be a worse Cuckold than you are, come away to the Joyners in Drury Lane, it being a convenient Bawdy-house, and you will find your Wife there, ready to add to your Horns.
Yours, Spywell.
—What means this? 'tis Bellamy's own hand.

ALITIA
How shall I come off now?—Why does not your Lordship see how excellent I am at counterfeiting hands? I fain'd Mr. Bellamy's Character, a purpose: It's not well.

LORD
This Woman's, false, I see't.—Who waits?

[Enter **PAGE**.

—Where's Bellamy.

PAGE
He has not been at home to night, my Lord.

ALITIA
I hope your Lordship will believe me now; but I was told he pay'd his visit to my Lady Thrivewell, this morning.

LORD
He is to receive money there for me, pray Heaven he be true, I scarce dare trust him. Tho I cannot believe what this false Woman says. Get my Coach ready, Ile go to Sir Olivers, my self.

ALITIA
I can tell you another circumstance of his dishonesty too.

LORD
What is't?

ALITIA
He loves, and is belov'd, (I mean dishonestly) by my Lady Thrivewell; and this he told me himself boastingly, that I might yeild the sooner.

LORD
Dare you justifie this?

ALITIA
Yes indeed, dare I to their faces.

LORD
And so you shall.—Mr. Saveall, your servant.

[Enter **SAVEALL**

SAVEALL
Mr. Bellamy, my Lord, is telling out the hundred pound at Sir Olivers, for you; but my Lord, there is a little difference in Sir Olivers Family, that my Lady desires your Lordship to compose, if possible.

LORD
With all my heart. My Coach:—You must along, Mrs. Saleware.

[Exit **LORD**, leading **MRS SALEWARE**, **TOM** and **SAVEALL**, follow.

SCENE: Changes To Sir Olivers House.

Enter **SIR OLIVER**, **LADY THRIVEWELL**, **CARELESS**, **PHEBE**, **CLOSETT**, and **WATT**.

SIR OLIVER
No, Villain, Ile have no more to do with thee. Ile leave thee to thy own shame and poverty.

CARELESS
It may be so.

SIR OLIVER
All that's thine, Ile turn out after thee; your Phebe, too, your virtuous Mistris, take her, and be gone.

CARELESS
I thank you for nothing, this was a moveable that belong'd to me, before your virtuous Wife lay'd us together.—Who the Devil wou'd have imagin'd, she shou'd have Gilted me so? a young hansome proper fellow as I am to?

SIR OLIVER
Sirrah, sirrah, have a care what you say of my Wife for I shall lay you fast enough else.

CARELESS
Is this—your witness, Sir; this pretious villain?

[Points to **WATT**.

WATT
No villain neither, Sir, since I have not betray'd my Master, for you turn'd me off basely.

CARELESS
Here's another of your Engins, this old Deceptio visus, that put me to Bed to the wrong Woman.

CLOSETT
Alas, good Gentleman,—ha, ha, ha.

CARELESS
But if, Mr. Bellamy, had been the Man, I suppose, Madam, you wou'd have kept your word; and old Mother Damnable, wou'd have brought the right party.

SIR OLIVER
What means he?

LADY
Fie, George, you'll be asham'd of this anon?

CARELESS
Faith, I shall not, and since you have betray'd me, I'll ruine you; therefore hear me, Oh thou credulous Knight, what I've to say unto thee.—

LADY
What canst thou say, good George, to my prejudice? Hold yet, whilst thy credit may be saved.

CARELESS
Not I, it shall out, unless you bribe me.

LADY
Not a farthing,—and see who'l have the worst on't.

SIR OLIVER
What would the Villain say to thy dishonour?

CARELESS
That, which if you are no contented Cuckold, will make you mad, Sir, it will:—you think I have done so lewd a thing in courting her,—but there's that smooth-fac'd young fellow, Bellamy, has courted her, and all the rest—I can assure you.

SIR OLIVER
Mr. Bellamy! it cannot be.

CARELESS
But it can, Sir; there's her procurer, old dark Lanthorn can tell you more.

CLOSETT
Who I? oh Lord!

CARELESS
Oh, she was chamber'd up with him at least two hours, a fair time,—under pretence of borrowing money; but you may guess his farther bus'ness, if you have any sense.

SIR OLIVER
I'l not believe this, Sir; 'tis malice.

CARELESS
'Tis fit you shou'd see't done, indeed, and great pity you did not.

SIR OLIVER
Oh, Mr. Saveall, if this be true, where's all my Reputation?—

CARELESS
And for that Rascal, Watt, there, I'l give you an account of him, which yet you never had: have you forgot, how we rescu'd you on Hounslow-heath, when you believ'd your self set on by Thieves?

SIR OLIVER
No, I have not forgot it; wou'd I had lost my Money nay a Limb, rather than have been by thee preserv'd.—

CARELESS
That project, Sir, was his, to get me into your favour again; the Robbers, as you thought 'em, were his acquaintance, Rogues of his managing, but to say truth, we meant no hurt, only I was forc'd, to colour the bus'ness, to give him a cut over the Pate, wou'd 't had kill'd him.

SIR OLIVER
Was't his Plot? I am glad to find him a fellow of that ingenuity: I love him for't.

CARELESS
Do you? then pray take notice, 'twas my own Plot, mine, Sir, to get my self into your favour.

WATT
Truly, Sir, my Master's in the right, 'twas his Plot.

SIR OLIVER
'Twas witty whose soe're 'twas, and I like it well, wou'd all the rest of the Actions of your life were as well.

CARELESS
Well, Sir, now you know my mind, and I'l take my leave; farewel, Nuncle. Come away, Phebe, I have been an unkind Dog to thee, that's truth: but come, I'l e'en make thee amends, and marry thee, and having no better way to live, e'en sell Coffee with thee.—Come away.—

[Offers to go.

LADY
Pray call him back; to let him go in this condition will undo him, and I desire to be clear'd too, before he goes of, the aspersion he has laid on me.

SIR OLIVER
Yes, Sir, you shall stay, and answer it before Authority.

CARELESS
Why, Sir, if you have a mind to have your house thought a Bawdy-house, I can stay, and prove it.

[Enter **CLOSETT**.

CLOSETT
Mrs. Crostil is come to wait on your Ladyship.

[Enter **MRS CROSTIL**, and a little after **CLARE** drest.

LADY
This is a great favour, Madam. Sir Oliver, pray entertain Mrs. Crostil a little.—

[**LADY** goes to **MRS CLARE** aside.

MRS CROSTILL

Methinks you all look disorder'd, I hope, Sir Oliver, you and your Nephew have a good understanding.

SIR OLIVER
No, Madam, nor do I desire to have any with such a Villain.

MRS CROSTILL
How, Sir? nay, if you rail at him 'twill make me love him.

SIR OLIVER
Then you are wretched.

MRS CROSTILL
Nay, then I'm resolv'd to love him—Pray what's she he makes such love to?

SIR OLIVER
A common wench, that's with child by him; she pleads a Contract with him, and he'l marry her.

MRS CROSTILL
Still you raise my flame to a greater height.—Mr. Careless, pray let me speak with you.

CARELESS
Who mean you, Madam,—me? I'm not at leisure now.

MRS CROSTILL
What the Duce was I made of, that his contempt of me increases my fire. Sir, I must needs speak with you.

CARELESS
What have you to say? Widow, you are come too late, Widow.

MRS CROSTILL
Pray walk a little this way,—I must speak to you alone.

[They go aside.

LADY
Pray keep your self conceal'd, my Lord will be
[To **CLARA**]
—here presently, and shall do you reason; he has mortgag'd a great part of his Estate to Sir Oliver, and the Forfeiture's out, and he shall be just to you, or we'l undo him.—Sir Oliver, pray whatever reason you have to be displeas'd with your Nephew your self, do not ruin his fortune with the widow.—
[Aside to **SIR OLIVER**]

CARELESS
Tempt me not, widow, to your own ruin, if I shou'd be so unlucky as to marry you, you are certainly undone, for I am one you cannot live with above a fortnight, you are fine limb'd and delicate, and I shall spoil you.—Here's one that knows my strength, and will hold me tack.—

MRS CROSTILL
I know not what you mean.

CARELESS
Nor prithee never try,—I advise you in time, widow, this wench here is only fit for me.

CARELESS
Is my profer'd passion scorn'd?—

CARELESS
Faith no, widow, but I shall never merit you:—besides, I am ingag'd, widow.

MRS CROSTILL
To that woman?—

CARELESS
Yes, to that woman; what exceptions have you to her?

MRS CROSTILL
Why she's a wench, a common prostitute.

CARELESS
Hark ye, have a care what you say (I advise you) before witness, do not abuse a woman I design to make a wife of, lest I hamper your Estate, widow.

MRS CROSTILL
She shall not be your wife, no woman but I shall marry you.

CARELESS
Have a care what you say before witness again, widow.

MRS CROSTILL
Call all to hear me, Sir Oliver, and the rest be witness I give my self to this Gentleman.—

CARELESS [To **PHEBE**]
Here's one forbids the Banes, widow.

MRS CROSTILL.
You shall compound with her.

CARELESS
But what said King Harry? Conscience,—conscience, widow.

MRS CROSTILL
No matter, Sir, give me your hand, beer witness all, I plight my Faith to this Gentleman.

SIR OLIVER
Then you are ruin'd.

MRS CROSTILL
Sir, 'tis too late to advise, I am resolv'd.

CARELESS
Have I caught you, widow,—hah, ha.—Farewel, Nuncle.—And yet—Conscience pulls me back.—Besides, widow, the woman is not satisfi'd.

MRS CROSTILL
I'll give her three hundred pound.

PHEBE
The woman is not such a fool to take it.

WATT
But the woman shall be so wise to take it, for what ever you all think, I do not love my Master so ill, to spoil his Fortune. And, Sir, truth is, I have receiv'd—some favors;—as they say, from Mrs. Phebe, as well as you, that is, she has been kind, Sir.

CARELESS
I thought so.

WATT
And I'm content to marry and make her honest, if she can get any addition to this Lady's bounty, to make her any fortune.

LADY
That was well said, Watt, and I'l promise the other hundred, in lieu of that I had in Wares of her Kinswoman, with your permission, Sir Oliver.

SIR OLIVER
With all my heart.

LADY
Watt, go for the Parson then, we'l have 'em married presently.

[Exit **WATT**.

[Enter **LORD**, **TOM SALEWARE**, and **ALITIA**.

LORD
Madam, in obedience to your commands, I am come to wait on you.

LADY
You have honor'd me, my Lord, tho our difference is almost at an end, yet I have something to deliver to your Lordship in private.

LORD

Madam, I have also a question to ask you in private too.

LADY
I shall be glad of any occasion to serve your Lordship.

LORD
Madam, will you withdraw a little? only this Gentlewoman may be witness of what I have to ask you.

LADY
I fancy what 'tis already, and must intreat your Lordship to speak it out, what e're it be.

LORD
'Twou'd not be for your Honor, Madam.

LADY
I am not of your opinion, my Lord, and that I may let you see I am not, I'l speak it for you: You come to ask me, and this woman to accuse me with dishonourable Love to a servant of yours, Bellamy I mean, is't not so?

LORD
Madam, it is.

LADY
This pleases me, indeed she has reveng'd her self handsomely, I have a Kinsman here of that opinion.

CARELESS
But, Madam, I recant, 'twas in the days of my debauch and brutality, I am reform'd now by your vertues only,—and humbly beg your pardon.

LORD
Madam, is not Bellamy, here?

LADY
He will be presently, my Lord, but now your Lordship, has question'd me, I hope I may have the same freedom with you?

LORD
Madam, you may command me any thing.

LADY
Pray where's my Sister Clara?

LORD
Is that a question for me to answer, Madam?

LADY
Yes, and which in Honour you are bound to answer: Did you not betray her to shame and infamy, and rob'd her of her Virgin purity?

LORD
I did not ravish her, Madam.

LADY
I do not say you did. But you had Flattery which did much more than force; I ask not her Honour back, but her life, and self, for we have never heard of her since that fatal Treachery of yours, and 'tis of you that I demand her.

LORD
You, cannot sure compel me to return her, if I cou'd?

CARELESS
But she shall, Sir, and I will be her Champion.

LORD
Her loss, Madam, is a greater Grief to me, than 'tis to you;—but for you, Sir, I shall find a time to try your prowess.

CLARA
But you shall not, Sir. Ile end the controversie.

LORD
I am amaz'd,—Clara,—and my Bellamy's the same.

LADY
Yes, your Bellamy, is the wrong'd Clara.—Do you not blush to see me?—I'm come to claim your vows, so often sworn, and so long broken.—

CARELESS
So, I was like to have made fine work.

ALITIA
Bless me! Bellamy, a Woman?

TOM
Never the sooner for a hasty word, I hope.

[Enter **WATT**.

WATT
Sir, the Parson's come.

CARELESS
Come, Widow, dare you sign, seal, and deliver?

MRS CROSTILL
With all my heart, Sir.

[Exit **CARELESS**, **WIDOW**, **WATT**, and **PHEBE**.

CLARA
Being by you undone, and made unfit to look abroad with Honour, and more unfit to live, but in the presence of you whom I ador'd; I did assume that Masculine habit, to let you see that I had rather live but by your sight alone, than be my self in any other part o'th' world; and by your sight alone, cou'd better contain my self, than she, the Mistris whom you so admir'd could, with the dear possession of you.

LORD
You melt my soul.—Pray let me make new vows to you, or well confirm the old.—

[Go aside.

ALITIA
Well, I am absolutely lost and undon in my Lords favor.

TOM
Never the sooner for a hasty word. Come, come, I do suspect this is all but a plot to make me jealous.

LADY
Wou'd you not be laught at now, sweet Mrs. Saleware?

TOM
No, indeed, Madam; nor shall she be by the proudest she that wears a head; or if she be, it will not make me jealous: Sapientia mea mihi, is my Motto still.

LADY
Yet I confess, this young Bellamy, and I have been bed-fellows some years since. Come be not out of countenance, I will not tell what my Husband did with you last term.

TOM
Nor shall you make me jealous, Madam, what'ere they did. Efacks not I, sweet ALITIA

LORD
Can you forgive what's past, and take a penitent man to your mercy?

LADY
My Lord, if you'll repair my Sisters honour, Sir Oliver, shall give you in your Mortgage?

LORD
'Tis all I wish on Earth to do so, Madam.

SIR OLIVER
Then, Sir, Ile restore your writings, and by it make her as good a Fortune as the Widow, and there's within a Parson shall end the difference.

LORD
It shall be done, Sir Oliver.
—For you, Mrs. Saleware, go home, look to your Shop, and please your Husband; for from this day, Ile never see you more.

ALITIA
I see all things are transitory,—and will turn Honest, and Thomas, you shall have no more fears of jealousie.

TOM
A Pox of Jealousie, I wish that were the worst grievance in the Nation, the jealousie that troubles my Noddle. No, no; Sapientia, &c. is my Motto.

[Enter **CARELESS, CROSTILL, WATT,** and **PHEBE**.

LADY
See, they are already Married.

TOM
What, my Cozin Phebe Gimcrack, too.—and 'efack, Ile take a frisk for joy. Watt get some Musick.

MRS CROSTILL
You shall not need, Sir, I have 'em at hand.

CARELESS
Well, Uncle, I hope we shall now be Friends, and according as I behave my self, let me have your favour,—you must all Dine with me to day; and at night, Widow—Ile say no more.—

SIR OLIVER
Well, Sir, as I shall see how you behave your self, I shall prove my self a loving Uncle.

CARELESS
I will be your Heir yet, in spight of ill Luck, and all my damn'd Debaucheries, which now farewell to.—

LORD
See, the Musick's here indeed, we'll lead the Bride a Dance, and then they shall do as much for us, Clara. They Dance all.

LORD
Now, Clare, that you and I may happy prove,
The Priest within shall consummate our Love.

[Exeunt.

Aphra Behn was baptised on December 14th in 1640.

Although she was a prolific and well established writer in her own lifetime facts about her remain scant and difficult to confirm. What can safely be said though is that Aphra Behn is now regarded as a key English playwright and a major figure in Restoration theatre

In fact even where and to whom she was born are subject to discussion.

According to which account you read – and there are many – Aphra was born in Harbledown, near Canterbury. Another that she was born to a barber, John Amis and his wife Amy. Or again she was born to a couple named Cooper.

In the "The Histories And Novels of the Late Ingenious Mrs. Behn" (1696) it is written that Aphra was born to Bartholomew Johnson, a barber, and Elizabeth Denham, a wet-nurse. However a claim by Colonel Thomas Colepeper, who states he knew her as a child, wrote in Adversaria that she was born at "Sturry or Canterbury" to a Mr Johnson and that she had a sister named Frances. Anne Kingsmill Finch, Countess of Winchilsea, a poetic contemporary, says that Aphra was born in Wye in Kent, and was the 'Daughter to a Barber.'

None of these accounts can be relied upon and it follows that with so few facts the early part of her life cannot be clearly illustrated.

However what can be accurately suggested is that Aphra was born in the rising tensions to the English Civil War. Obviously a time of much division and difficulty as the King and Parliament, and their respective forces, came ever closer to conflict.

But still facts do not reveal themselves in any quantity. As a young woman a version exists of Aphra's journeying to Surinam with Bartholomew Johnson. He was said to have died on the journey, leaving his wife and children spending some months in the country. It is during this trip that Aphra claims to have met an African slave leader. These experiences formed the basis for one of her most famous works, "Oroonoko". In "Oroonoko" Behn Aphra gifts herself the position of narrator and her first biographer accepted the proposition that Aphra was indeed the daughter of the lieutenant general of Surinam, as in the story. There is little evidence to support this case, and none of her contemporaries acknowledge this, or any, aristocratic status. There is also no evidence that Oroonoko existed as an actual person or that any such slave revolt, is anything but an invention.

However it is possible that she acted a spy in the colony. Possibilities exist. Perhaps Aphra re-wrote her own history as and when it suited her needs at the time.

The common method of gathering information in these times was Church records and for a few, tax records. Aphra Behn is mentioned in neither. As well as Aphra Behn or Mrs Behn she was, at times, also known as Ann Behn, Mrs Bean, agent 160 and Astrea.

Shortly after her supposed return to England from Surinam in 1664, Aphra may have married Johan Behn (also written as Johann and John Behn). He could have been a merchant of German or Dutch extraction, possibly from Hamburg. He died or the couple separated that same year, however from this point we can be sure Aphra used the title "Mrs Behn" as her professional name.

There is some suggestion that Aphra may have been a Catholic or at least leaned towards this school of faith. She once commented that she was "designed for a nun." Many of those around her were Catholic, such as Henry Neville who was later arrested for his Catholicism, and this would have aroused suspicions during the anti-Catholic fervour of the 1680s. She was a monarchist, and her sympathy for the Stuarts, and particularly for the Catholic Duke of York may be demonstrated by her dedication of her play "The Rover, Part II" to him after he had been exiled for the second time. Aphra was dedicated to the restored King Charles II. As political parties emerged during this time, Aphra became a Tory supporter.

By 1666 Aphra had become attached to the court. Domestically the Plague was sweeping the Nation and the Great Fire was about to erupt through London. In foreign affairs England and the Netherlands had engaged in The Second Anglo-Dutch War from 1665. Aphra was recruited as a political spy in Antwerp on behalf of King Charles II, possibly in league with Thomas Killigrew.

This is probably the beginning of more accurate records on Aphra's life. Her code name is said to have been Astrea (though there are others), a name under which she later published many of her writings. Her chief duty was to establish a relationship with William Scot, son of Thomas Scot, a regicide who had been executed in 1660. Scot was believed to be ready to become a spy in the English service and to report on the activities of the English exiles who were thought to be plotting against the King. Aphra arrived in Bruges in July 1666 with a mission to secure Scot into a double agent, but there is evidence that Scot would betray her to the Dutch.

Aphra however found life as a spy not quite the romantic interlude that many assume would be the case. She arrived unprepared; the cost of living shocked her, and after a month, she had to pawn her jewellery. King Charles was slow in paying, either for her services or for her expenses whilst abroad. She had to borrow money so she could return to London, where she spent a year petitioning King Charles for payment unsuccessfully. A short while later a warrant was issued for her arrest, but little to suggest it was actually served or that she went to prison for her debt.

The death of her husband and her debts seemed to push her towards a more sustainable and substantial career. Aphra began work for the King's Company and the Duke's Company players as a scribe. These were, in fact, the only two licensed theatre groups in London. The theatres had been closed under Cromwell and were now re-opening under Charles II and a more liberal atmosphere. Theatre technology was being imported from Europe and being integrated into the staging of some plays. It was a great moment on which to embark upon a career in theatre.

Aphra who had previously only written poetry now embarked on such a career. Her first, "The Forc'd Marriage", was staged in 1670, followed by "The Amorous Prince" (1671). After her third play, "The Dutch Lover", fails to please Aphra had a three year lull in her writing career. Again it is speculated that she went travelling again, possibly once again as a spy.

After this sojourn her writing moves towards comic works, which prove commercially more successful. Her most popular works included "The Rover" and "Love-Letters Between a Nobleman and His Sister" (1684–87).

With her growing reputation Aphra became friends with many of the most notable writers of the day. This is The Age of Dryden and his literary dominance. As well as his friendship she includes also those of Elizabeth Barry, John Hoyle, Thomas Otway and Edward Ravenscroft, and was also attached to the circle of the Earl of Rochester.

Aphra often used her plays to attack the parliamentary Whigs claiming, "In public spirits call'd, good o' th' Commonwealth... So tho' by different ways the fever seize...in all 'tis one and the same mad disease." This was Aphra's criticism to parliament which had denied the king funds.

From the mid 1680's Aphra's health began to decline. This was exacerbated by her continual state of debt and descent into poverty.

In 1687 she published A Discovery of New Worlds, a translation of a French popularisation of astronomy, Entretiens sur la pluralité des mondes, by Bernard le Bovier de Fontenelle, written as a novel in a form similar to her own work, but with her new, religiously oriented preface.

As her end approached in 1689 it became increasingly hard for her to even hold a pen though her desire to continue to write was unquenchable. In her final days, she wrote the translation of the final book of Abraham Cowley's Six Books of Plants.

Aphra Behn died on April 16th 1689, and is buried in the East Cloister of Westminster Abbey. The inscription on her tombstone reads: "Here lies a Proof that Wit can never be Defence enough against Mortality." She was quoted as stating that she had led a "life dedicated to pleasure and poetry."

Her legacy is broad. Firstly as a woman she broke down many of the barriers which regarded only men as writers, especially in the commercial arena. In all she would write and have performed 19 plays, contribute to more, and become one of the first prolific, high-profile female dramatists in these Isles.

In her own golden age of the 1670s and 1680s she was one of the most productive playwrights in Britain, second only to the immense talents of the Poet Laureate John Dryden.

Much of her work has been criticised for its bawdy tone as well as its masculine form but needs must and she was working to live, to survive, and to widen her spread as an author.

She received widespread support from many other successful writers including Thomas Otway, Nahum Tate (also a Poet Laureate), Jacob Tonson, Nathaniel Lee and Thomas Creech.

Aphra is now rightly seen as a key dramatist of the seventeenth-century theatre. Her prose vitally important to the on-going development of the English novel.

Following Aphra's death new female dramatists such as 'Ariadne', Delarivier Manley, Mary Fix, Susanna Centlivre and Catherine Trotter acknowledged Behn as an inspiration who opened up the public space for women writers to be accepted.

In succeeding centuries her appreciation has been volatile. For instance in the morally reserved Victorian clime both the writer and her works were ignored or dismissed as indecent. The Victorian novelist and critic Julia Kavanagh wrote, "the disgrace of Aphra Behn is that, instead of raising man to woman's moral standard, she sank woman to the level of man's coarseness".

However by the 20th century, however, Aphra's fame was back in fashion. Since then her works have been well appreciated and her place in our literary pantheon assured.

Aphra Behn – A Concise Bibliography

Plays
The Forced Marriage (1670)
The Amorous Prince (1671)
The Dutch Lover (1673)
Abdelazer (1676)
The Town Fop (1676)
The Rover, Part I (1677)
Sir Patient Fancy (1678)
The Feigned Courtesans (1679)
The Young King (1679)
The False Count (1681)
The Rover, Part II (1681)
The Roundheads (1681)
The City Heiress (1682)
Like Father, Like Son (1682)
Prologue and Epilogue to Romulus and Hersilia, or The Sabine War (November 1682)
The Lucky Chance (1686) with composer John Blow
The Emperor of the Moon (1687)
The Widow Ranter (1689)
The Younger Brother (1696)

Novels
The Fair Jilt
Agnes de Castro
Love-Letters Between a Nobleman and His Sister (1684)
Oroonoko (1688)

Short Stories
The Fair Jilt (1688)
The History of the Nun: or, the Fair Vow-Breaker (1688)
The History of the Servant
The Lover-Boy of Germany
The Girl Who Loved the German Lover-Boy

Poetry Collections
Poems upon Several Occasions, with A Voyage to the Island of Love (1684)
Lycidus; or, The Lover in Fashion (1688)

www.ingramcontent.com/pod-product-compliance
Lightning Source LLC
Chambersburg PA
CBHW051700040426
42446CB00009B/1232